insight text guide

Jane McGennisken

Life of Galileo

Bertolt Brecht

First published in 1999. This 2nd edition published in 2013, reprinted 2014, 2015 (twice).

Insight Publications Pty Ltd
3/350 Charman Road
Cheltenham VIC 3192
Australia
Tel: +61 3 8571 4950
Fax: +61 3 8571 0257
Email: books@insightpublications.com.au

www.insightpublications.com.au

National Library of Australia Cataloguing-in-Publication entry:

McGennisken, Jane.
Bertolt Brecht's life of Galileo / Jane McGennisken.
2nd ed.
9781922150783 (pbk.)
Insight text guide.
Includes bibliographical references.
Secondary school students.
Brecht, Bertolt, 1898–1956. Life of Galileo.
Brecht, Bertolt, 1898–1956. —Criticism and interpretation.
832.912

Other ISBNs:

9781925175110 (digital)
9781925175448 (bundle: print + digital)

Cover design: The Modern Art Production Group

Printed in Australia.

contents

CHARACTER MAP

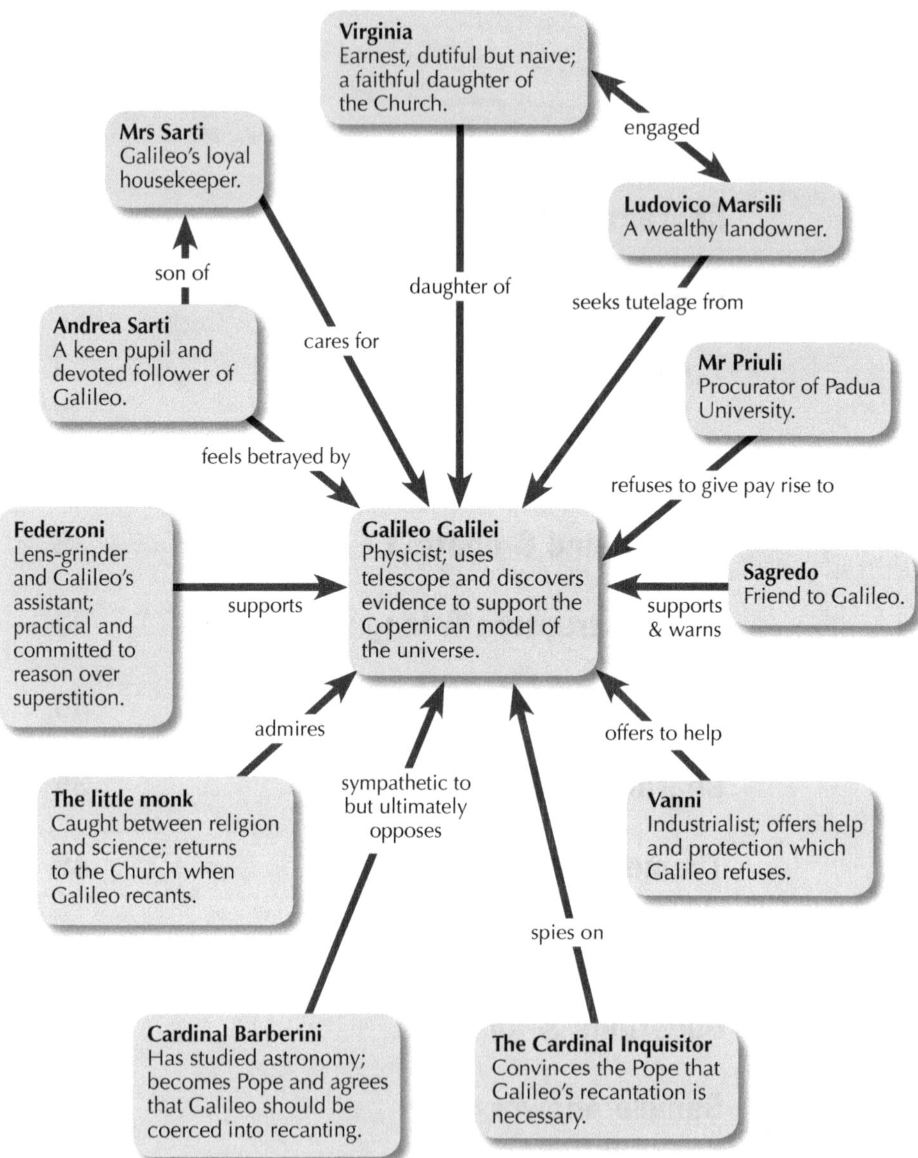

OVERVIEW

About the author

Bertolt Brecht is an historically significant playwright, so much so that the term 'Brechtian theatre' has been coined in connection with his work. Indeed, he is arguably one of the most influential forces in Western theatre since World War II. Brecht's theory of, and experiments with, epic theatre sought to dismantle the illusion of naturalistic theatre by drawing attention to its artifice: the so-called 'fourth wall'. (For further information about epic theatre, see the 'Genre' section of this guide.) In many ways, Brecht's concern with critical seeing (the interrogation of what lies beneath appearances) can be largely attributed to the times in which he lived.

Born Eugen Berthold Friedrich Brecht in Germany in 1898, he attended Augsburg Grammar School. He was not an especially notable student, apart from the anti-establishment ideas he was already forming. Biographical synopses of Brecht's life often make note of his near expulsion after he wrote an essay disputing the patriotic line 'It is a sweet and honourable thing to die for one's country' (Rorrison 1986, p.v). In 1918 (the year following the Russian Revolution), Brecht, by this time a medical student, was conscripted and served as a medical orderly during World War I.

By 1927 Brecht was becoming a recognisable force in the theatre. He maintained his interest in politics and began studying Marx in the 1920s. These two interests intersected so that his plays often reflected overtly political agendas, themes and ideas. When the Nazis won power in 1933, Brecht was forced to flee Germany. While living in exile in Denmark, Sweden and Finland, Brecht wrote his teaching or 'parable' plays in which he portrayed abstract political and moral themes in historically and geographically distant contexts. In settings carefully removed from their immediate environments, his audiences were forced to confront moral questions relevant to their own times. *Life of Galileo* is one of these 'epic masterpieces' (Stanton and Banham 1996, p.43). Originally written in 1938, the play was revised three times to reflect Brecht's changing views on science and politics – especially the social responsibility of the scientist. (For further information on this revision process, see the 'Different Interpretations' section of this guide.)

In 1941 Brecht emigrated to the United States and in 1945 he completed an English version of *Life of Galileo* with American actor Charles Laughton. At this time, Brecht's original characterisation of Galileo, in which Galileo was a flawed yet positive figure who outsmarted an authoritarian regime, underwent a fairly radical reimagining. Galileo was subsequently presented as a weak and self-serving symbol of scientific hubris. Of course, such a revision of the central character was directly connected to Brecht's experiences of World War II, especially the atrocities committed under the guise of scientific research in Nazi Germany. The arrival of the atomic age and the bombing of Hiroshima and Nagasaki gave rise to yet another revision.

In a parallel with Galileo's experiences before the Inquisition, Brecht was called to appear before the House Un-American Activities Committee. Before he had the chance to see the American version of *Life of Galileo* on stage in New York, Brecht left America due to his concern about the pervasive anti-Communist sentiment gripping the country. In 1948 Brecht returned to East Berlin, establishing the Berliner Ensemble in the following year with his wife, Helene Weigel. The ensemble was very successful, and was pivotal in firmly establishing Brecht's influence on contemporary theatre. Brecht died in 1956 before seeing *Life of Galileo* open at the Berliner Ensemble in 1957.

Synopsis

With the help of a Dutch invention, the telescope, the central character, Galileo, finds evidence to support the Copernican system. Galileo wants to share this knowledge but does not recognise (or refuses to acknowledge) how this might affect the teachings and authority of the Catholic Church, a powerful institution and, indeed, the ideological arm of the ruling class. Despite warnings to the contrary, Galileo goes to Florence and thence to Rome to share his discoveries and to secure funding for further research.

Although the Church representatives at the Collegium Romanum the apex of Jesuit education agree that Galileo is right in his observations, they do not wish this to become public knowledge. Galileo agrees to research less-threatening propositions and does not publicise his findings about the system of the universe.

When a mathematician is made pope, Galileo optimistically believes that his discoveries will now be welcome. He publishes *Dialogue Concerning the Two Chief World Systems*, but things do not turn out as Galileo imagines and the Church gives him a choice: face torture or recant.

The Cardinal Inquisitor has merely to show Galileo the torture instruments to induce him to make a public statement disavowing his earlier theories. However, unbeknownst to the Church, while under house arrest he secretly copies his research so that it can be disseminated among the scientific community. When his former student Andrea comes to visit, Galileo gives him the *Discorsi* to smuggle out of the country.

Character summaries

Life of Galileo calls for a large cast of characters. Rather than summarising every character in the play, as some are so minor as to be inconsequential, the following list includes the key players.

Galileo Galilei

Central character; self-centred, brilliant mathematician who likes the good things in life. For Galileo, the pursuit of new knowledge is an addiction. He sees the new model of the universe as the dawn of a new age, both for science and society. Initially presented in a sympathetic light, Galileo is condemned when he falls far short of his ideals. Ultimately, Galileo is an ambiguous figure.

Andrea Sarti

Son of Galileo's housekeeper; a bright student, his respect for his hero is shattered when Galileo recants. However, when Galileo commissions him to smuggle the *Discorsi* across the border, Andrea's faith in his mentor is restored.

Mrs Sarti

Galileo's housekeeper and mother of Andrea; sensible, loyal and honest, she cares about Galileo, but does not approve of his new theories. Exits the play at the end of Scene 9.

Ludovico Marsili

Member of the wealthy and powerful landowning class; when Galileo refuses to drop his research, Ludovico breaks off his engagement to Galileo's daughter, Virginia.

The Procurator (Mr Priuli)

Bursar; sees everything according to business principles; agrees to a pay increase for Galileo in exchange for the telescope; is angry when similar Dutch instruments flood the market.

Sagredo

Friend of Galileo; loyal and honest; warns Galileo about leaving the safety of independent Venice for monk-run Florence.

Virginia

Galileo's daughter; superstitious and prayerful; often overlooked, especially by her father; doomed when he destroys her engagement; ends up an old maid and her father's gaoler.

Federzoni

Lens-grinder and Galileo's assistant; man of science and reason; one of Galileo's disciples.

The Doge

Elected leader of the Republic of Venice; makes a minor appearance in Scene 2 to tell Galileo that the city rewards scholars who contribute to its prosperity.

Senators

Representatives of the self-interest of the ruling class (Scene 2).

Cosimo de Medici

The Grand Duke of Florence; in Scene 4, aged nine, isn't allowed to look through the telescope; reappears in Scene 11 when he refuses to accept Galileo's book.

The court chamberlain

Court official; officious, superficial; concerned only with getting Cosimo back in time for the court ball.

The theologian

One of the short-sighted Florentine scholars who visits Galileo's house.

The philosopher

Supercilious; refuses to see the evidence before his eyes; frightened about where the truth might lead.

The mathematician

Like the philosopher, refuses to look through the telescope; horrified that Galileo dares to question the foundational science and philosophy of Aristotle.

Two nuns

Embody the antithesis of charity and kindness; hurry away from Galileo when they realise he has been in contact with the plague.

Two soldiers

Indifferent to human suffering; just doing their jobs.

The old woman

Sympathetic; defends the city officials who are 'powerless' in the face of the plague.

A fat prelate

Mocks Galileo and his ideas.

Two scholars

Cheapen and sensationalise Galileo's theories, for laughs.

Two monks

Like the others in the Collegium Romanum, they belittle Galileo.

Two astronomers

Resistant to new ideas and change; happy to accept that humans cannot understand everything.

A very thin monk

Fanatical, takes the Scriptures literally.

The very old cardinal

Fundamentalist; subscribes to an anthropocentric (human-centred) view of the universe.

Father Christopher Clavius

Church expert in astronomy; confirms Galileo's findings; so arrogant and powerful that he doesn't look at anyone as he passes through the hall.

The little monk

Conflicted; torn between reason and faith. Studies with and admires Galileo but returns to the Church when Galileo recants.

The Cardinal Inquisitor

Suspicious, controlling; views Galileo as dangerous and his book a heresy; convinces the Pope he must show Galileo instruments of torture to make him recant.

Cardinal Barberini, subsequently Pope Urban VIII

Mathematician; sympathetic to Galileo's thirst for knowledge. Ultimately, a man of the Church, not science.

Cardinal Bellarmin

Elegant, sophisticated and powerful; embodies qualities of the ruling classes.

Two clerical secretaries

Uphold the old order, as illustrated by the way they play chess and by their records of Galileo's conversations for the Inquisitor.

Filippo Mucius

Galileo's former student; publishes work refuting the Copernican system.

Mr Gaffone

Rector of the University of Pisa.

The ballad singer and his wife

Appear in the carnival scene; sing about the upside down world caused by Galileo's Copernican research.

Vanni

Member of the rising manufacturing classes; rational-minded; offers Galileo safety and protection.

An official; a high official

Demonstrate Galileo's fall from favour by their rude treatment of Virginia and Galileo; announce that the Florentine court cannot protect Galileo.

An individual

Secret policeman of the Inquisition.

A frontier guard

Permits Andrea to leave Italy with Galileo's *Discorsi*.

A clerk

Superficially checks Andrea's books and writings at the border; sees nothing of concern.

BACKGROUND & CONTEXT

Galileo Galilei and the scientific revolution

The play is based on the life of Galileo Galilei (1564–1642) who was a key figure in the scientific revolution of the seventeenth century. Through modifications of the telescope, Galileo was able to make observations that demonstrated that the earth and other planets revolve around the sun, thus confirming the Copernican system of astronomy. Such a system did not correspond to the Bible's description of the origins of the universe.

This proof was a significant challenge to accepted thinking, particularly in connection with the teachings of the Roman Catholic Church. Before the Copernican system was posited, the Church and its believers understood that the universe was geocentric. In other words, the sun was supposed to revolve around the earth. The original proponent of this view, Aristotle (384–322 BCE), was an ancient Greek scientist and philosopher. Aristotle conceived an ordered universe divided into two chief parts: the earth (a place of change and corruption) and the heavens (unchanging perfection). Importantly, Aristotle's cosmos was finite; nothing existed beyond the known universe. In the cosmology described by Aristotle a series of spherical shells neatly fitted inside each other. Each spherical shell contained a heavenly body or bodies – the Moon, Mercury, Venus, Sun, Mars, Jupiter, Saturn and the fixed stars. As these shells or spheres turned, so too did the body within it.

However, the universe described by Aristotle did not always correlate with the observable movement of the planets. Clearly, this presented a significant problem for astronomy. Even though the spherical cosmology described by Aristotle survived until the seventeenth century, mathematicians had to create a complicated system of geometrical models to accommodate the ways in which the planets actually moved. To this end, Claudius Ptolemy (c. 150 CE) developed the Ptolemaic system. Even though this slightly altered the laws of Aristotle's original explanation of the universe, it managed to marry together the essential elements of the biblical and the visible universe.

During the Renaissance, when astronomers began attempting to model the movement of the stars according to mathematical principles, the Ptolemaic system became increasingly untenable. In 1543, the Polish astronomer Nicolaus Copernicus published his theory placing the sun at the centre of the universe. A stationary sun and moving earth conflicted with many biblical passages and, for the Church, this was to become increasingly problematic. When Giordano Bruno adopted the Copernican system to describe God as universal and within all things, rather than a person, the Catholic Church saw how Copernicus' theory might undermine the Scriptures and Church authority. Subsequently, in 1616, his book was placed on the Church's 'Index of Forbidden Books'. At the same time, the head of the Holy Office of the Inquisition, Cardinal Robert Bellarmine, warned Galileo not to defend or teach Copernican theory.

In 1632, Galileo's *Dialogue Concerning the Two Chief World Systems* attacked the physics and cosmology of Aristotle and the astronomy of Ptolemy. Using his telescope, Galileo had been able to see the peaks and valleys of the moon, discover the four satellites of Jupiter, observe the phases of Venus and detect the existence of sunspots. Galileo's telescopic observations added considerable weight to his arguments.

The implications of these new scientific discoveries were significant. If, as Galileo suggested, the Bible and Aristotle's laws of physics were proven incorrect in relation to the structure of the universe, what other key tenets of the Faith could be called into question? In this sense, Galileo's research threatened to undermine world views and, by extension, even the contemporary social structure.

In 1633, the Inquisition called Galileo to Rome and he was subsequently found guilty of heresy. He was placed under house arrest for the remainder of his life. By 1638 Galileo was totally blind and in 1642 he died at his home outside Florence.

Brecht's historical context and political views

As the preceding section about Galileo Galilei's historical context attests, there is often a great tension between those who think and act outside the social and ideological 'norms' and those who belong to the establishment (whether such an 'establishment' is formalised through governmental structures or constituted by an imagined community). Similarly, Bertolt Brecht lived during a period of tumultuous and rapid change in which religious and political views and sympathies were sometimes used as justification for persecution. In this sense, there are some significant historical parallels between the two men and their experiences.

Brecht's political allegiances (he had begun to study Karl Marx's *Das Kapital* in 1926) meant that he had hoped for the dawn of a new age following the First World War. Indeed, Brecht had dreamed of a socialist state in Germany like the one created during the Russian Revolution of 1917. Of course, by the time Brecht fled Germany in the early 1930s, the rise of Hitler had cruelly dashed any such hopes for the future of his homeland. Significantly, Brecht wrote *Life of Galileo,* originally with the title *The Earth Moves,* against a backdrop of impending war. At the time, November 1938, Brecht was living in Denmark, having experienced firsthand the terror and dislocation of flight and exile as he escaped the increasingly powerful Third Reich. In 1939 Brecht made minor revisions to the play with the new title of *Life of Galileo.*

In witnessing political oppression and the often-clandestine ways in which people resisted such oppression, Brecht saw in the character of Galileo a figure of hope for the future. Just as Galileo had managed to outmanoeuvre the powerful authorities of seventeenth-century Italy, Brecht's contemporaries sought ways to undermine the Nazi regime. Rather than becoming a martyr, Galileo survived and secretly bided his time so that he could ensure the survival of his work (that would, ultimately, result in seismic shifts in the social order). During his own exile, Brecht clearly felt some correspondence with Galileo's plight and in his writing voiced his personal opposition to events unfolding in Nazi Germany.

Another significant influence on the later version of Brecht's play was the role of science in World War II, especially the splitting of the atom and its implications for contemporary warfare – for example, the bombing of Hiroshima and Nagasaki. This new concern led to another revision of the play in August 1945 – an English translation, in partnership with the actor Charles Laughton. Instead of portraying Galileo as a visionary whose scientific research might improve the lot of the people, he was recast as an immoral and weak man. In Galileo, the father of a new system of physics, Brecht (perhaps unfairly) found a scapegoat for the atomic age and its disastrous consequences. Galileo became the individual responsible for leading science down a terrible path in which technological knowledge and advancement became mere tools for the ruling classes. In Brecht's view, Galileo was responsible for this tragic decline in scientific morals and standards, and he revised the play (and the character) to better reflect this condemnation. His vision of Galileo was significantly tainted by evidence of Nazi Germany's abuse of science, such as its practice of engaging in medical research on human subjects.

The Cold War

Ideological battles continued to be fought following World War II. For Brecht, interested in Galileo's story because of the differing ideologies it represented, the ensuing Cold War presented further examples of Inquisition-style politics and betrayals. Brecht was living in exile in America for a time during this period.

The Cold War refers to the arms race between the Soviet Union (under Stalin) and the United States, in which the conflict between two different political systems (communism and democracy) resulted in espionage and nuclear weapons research and development. In the United States during this period, diverse political views were no longer tolerated and Russian Communism was posited as the enemy of Western capitalism and of democratic principles. Brecht was caught up in this maelstrom of political unrest when he was called before the

House Un-American Activities Committee (HUAC). The committee, formed in 1938, had begun by investigating Communist infiltration into the American administration but became a more dangerous force in 1945 with its power continuing well into the 1950s. Brecht was called before HUAC in 1947 where he was expected to account for his Communist tendencies. Originally, Brecht, as one of eleven 'unfriendly' witnesses, had refused to give evidence about his political beliefs and activities. In October, however, Brecht did appear before HUAC. He was so disturbed by this experience, and the way in which America was increasingly framing Communism in hostile and fearful ways, that he flew to Switzerland shortly after his testimony. He did not see the New York performance of *Galileo*.

After fifteen years of exile, Brecht returned to Germany to live in East Berlin where he and his wife, Helene Weigel, started up the state-subsidised and highly successful theatre company, the Berliner Ensemble. During the 1950s, Brecht maintained his interest in what was happening elsewhere in the world and it is hardly surprising that he continued to view *Life of Galileo* as relevant and topical when it went into rehearsals in 1956. In 1953, Ethel and Julius Rosenberg had been executed in the United States for betraying atomic secrets to the Russians; in 1954 Robert J. Oppenheimer, an atomic physicist, was put on trial in America, in yet another kind of inquisition. During a superpower arms race, and amidst a climate of fear and suspicion, Brecht's play as a potential warning about the social responsibility of the scientist was particularly pertinent.

Brecht died in 1956; the third and final version of *Life of Galileo* opened at the Berliner Ensemble in 1957.

GENRE, STRUCTURE & LANGUAGE

Genre

This play can be considered as belonging to more than one theatrical genre; Brecht used various elements to suit his overall purpose and to create a complex portrayal of historical figures and events.

The history play

Life of Galileo can be regarded as a history play because it is based on events drawn from a particular period in the past. Indeed, in writing about the last stage of the Renaissance, Brecht borrows one of its forms, the Shakespearean History, to present his play. As the critic M. A. Cohen puts it:

> Brecht is assuming, like his Elizabethan counterparts, that the function of history is didactic: we have both a modern preoccupation with authenticity and a neo-Elizabethan desire to use the past to point morals for the present. (Cohen 1970, p.81)

Of course, Brecht alters some historical details to better fit his theatrical vision. For example, the Galileo of the play has only one daughter, Virginia, even though historically he had three children. Virginia's engagement to Ludovico is entirely invented. Similarly, some dates and corresponding time frames have been changed. However, the play largely corresponds to the record of Galileo's life and most biographical details are authentic.

The parable or 'teaching' play

In some ways, *Life of Galileo* can also be categorised according to its didactic 'teaching' purpose. In this sense the play operates as a parable or exemplum, a story that endorses certain values while simultaneously warning against others. In this case the audience is supposed to take something away from the play. It is meant not to be simply a pleasurable experience, but to make the audience think and reflect critically on the themes, issues and ideas it presents.

Epic theatre

Considering *Life of Galileo* in terms of how it fulfils the expectations of a parable play necessarily leads to a discussion of Brecht's conceptualisation of epic theatre. Epic theatre grew out of the social and artistic contexts in which it was conceived; it was a reaction to the focus on emotion found in expressionism. In a 1927 newspaper article, Brecht pronounced, 'The essential point of the epic theatre is perhaps that it appeals less to the feelings than to the spectator's reason' (Stanton & Banham 1996, p.110). In this sense, the audience is positioned to reflect rationally on the performance rather than be carried away by it.

In 1931 Brecht formalised the conventions of this emerging theatrical style when he outlined the contrasts between dramatic and epic theatre. Whereas dramatic theatre provides a spectator with sensations and experience, epic theatre forces the spectator to face an issue and thereby arouses a desire to take action. Compared to the traditionally linear style of development in dramatic theatre, where one scene leads to another and where the audience is focused on the finish, each scene in epic theatre is a more self-contained 'vignette'; subsequently, spectators are not so interested in a cumulative end goal. In Brecht's epic theatre, the human being is portrayed as a process rather than a fixed point (in other words, the human being can change). Critical distance is crucial because the audience needs to be alert to the way in which events are unfolding so that they can judge whether or not this is the 'right' way of things.

Life of Galileo does not properly fit the mould of epic theatre, although it does incorporate a few key features of this form. These features, and how they do or do not correspond to epic theatre, will be considered below in the section on structure.

Structure

Although Brecht suggested that epic theatre should move in large-scale curves and jumps (rather than in a straightforward, linear fashion), *Life of Galileo* is structured according to more conventional dramatic techniques. The play covers twenty-six years chronologically, in a sequence of fifteen scenes depicting pivotal events in Galileo's life. Brecht does, however, move Galileo's research on sunspots forward by ten years so that it has the dramatic effect of coinciding with the appointment of the new pope.

In epic theatre, to draw attention to the play's constructed nature, characters occasionally step out of their roles and a commentator expresses thoughts about the unfolding action. This does not occur in *Life of Galileo*; however, Brecht does include captions and verse summaries before each scene to inform the audience of what is about to happen. These can be displayed or read aloud during performance. The captions have the effect of dismantling theatrical illusion: the audience does not pleasurably wait in anticipation and suspense because everybody already knows what is to occur. In this way, the audience can concentrate on the scene as a 'demonstration' or lesson. Audience members are expected to objectively judge Galileo's words and actions.

A note on staging

In keeping with Brecht's ideas about epic theatre, a sparse set design is usually employed for *Life of Galileo*. As Brecht did not want audience members to be seduced by the idea that they were looking into a real room, the setting is suggested by a largely empty and neutral space that includes only a few key props. This deliberately draws attention to the contrived dramatic space of the theatre (in the absence of anything elaborately 'realistic'). In this way, the staging of the play can fulfil some of the requirements of the epic theatre form that are otherwise absent in the script itself.

Q What props would you use to indicate the different settings in this play? Consider props of symbolic significance. (For example, how might you portray the relative wealth and power of the Collegium Romanum?)

Language

Characterisation, or personality, is created by the actions of characters (stage directions), the physical places in which they move (setting) and by both what they say and what others say about them (language). Therefore, the language used by the various characters, not just what they say but also the manner in which they say it, helps the audience to understand how to read or interpret the character and their motives. It is crucial to analyse language to understand a character's values and beliefs (and the way we, as responders to the text, are being positioned to view these same values and beliefs).

Galileo is a man of science and learning, which is reflected in his vocabulary (his choice of words) and the more academic, measured arguments he presents (the way he puts his words together). This is established in the first scene of the play during the exchange between Galileo and Andrea. When Andrea refers to the milkman 'making' a circle around the house because he has not been paid, Galileo corrects him: 'Describing a circle, you mean, Andrea' (p.5). Just as Galileo's language here reveals something about his exacting nature, it also says a great deal about the relationship he has with Andrea. As Andrea's mentor, he is respectful of the boy's intelligence and abilities and corrects him in a teacherly manner. Similarly, when Andrea asks about a wooden model of the Ptolemaic system, Galileo again draws on scientific language to suggest a deductive and rational research method to enable his student to grasp its significance: 'Let's examine it. Start at the beginning. Description?' (p.6).

The language that Galileo uses when talking to and about his own daughter is also instructive. In Scene 3, when Galileo wonders whether the Florentine court will have him, Virginia's response reveals that she is eager to please, and possibly a little vacuous. She says, 'Of course they'll have you, Father, with your new stars and all that' (p.32). In referring to Galileo's very serious research as 'new stars and all that', Virginia's language use portrays her as empty-headed and not especially discerning in her word choice. It is the precise opposite of Galileo's ordered way of speaking of the universe. Their different values and estranged relationship are neatly encapsulated here. After her well-meant but clearly valueless assurance, Galileo very dismissively tells Virginia to 'Run along to your mass' (p.32).

A note on translations

Life of Galileo was originally written in German (1938–9). In the second, American version, it was revised and translated into English (1946–7). Finally, the play was retranslated back into German. Presumably, as part of the translation process, *Life of Galileo* has been altered in some ways. Interestingly, in his introduction to Brecht's *Parables of the Theatre*, Eric Bentley comments that English translations from German are always shorter than the original. While this can mean only minor changes to a text, there are occasions when 'translation becomes adaptation' (Bentley 1965, p.16). This is important when studying *Life of Galileo* because the translator is central to the English language version we read. The translator must weigh one word against another, or indeed, one phrase against another, to maintain the style of the play.

SCENE-BY-SCENE ANALYSIS

Scene 1 (pp.5–19)

Summary: *Galileo Galilei, a mathematics teacher at Padua University, explains to his housekeeper's son that he intends to prove Copernicus' theory that the earth revolves around the sun. He has two visitors: Ludovico, who seeks tutelage, and the university procurator who refuses Galileo's request for a wage increase.*

This scene introduces some of the key characters and sets up several of the important ideas and themes that are explored throughout *Life of Galileo*. At the outset, Galileo's exchange with Andrea is instructive. In the supportive way of a father teaching a son, Galileo insists that Andrea uses scientific and mathematical terminology in his everyday observations. Galileo clearly respects Andrea's intellect and spends some time questioning him about the Ptolemaic system before reintroducing a discussion, from the previous day, of Copernicus' hypothesis.

A new world of knowledge

Most significantly, in this discussion Galileo reveals his excitement about a new world of knowledge in which scientific discoveries and new ways of seeing undermine tired and outdated ideas. Galileo proclaims: 'Our cities are cramped, and so are men's minds. Superstition and the plague. But now the word is "that's how things are, but they won't stay like that". Because everything is in motion, my friend' (p.6).

Galileo's proposed model of the movement of the earth (following the Copernican theory) is symbolic of the way world views themselves are moving and changing. The contemporary social structure, Galileo believes, will not withstand the revolutions in scientific thinking. Note the active language and verbs sprinkled throughout Galileo's speech. Now, Galileo argues, people are 'breaking out' of immobility, they have 'ventured out across the seas' and a 'draught … is blowing up the gold-embroidered skirts of the prelates and princes' (pp.6–7). This also reflects Brecht's concern with social change and class structure.

Two and two makes five

When Mrs Sarti (Andrea's mother and Galileo's housekeeper) overhears their discussions she says, 'you'll have Andrea believing two and two makes five any minute now' (p.9). This is significant because there are a number of references throughout the play to quantifiable, observable phenomena that can either prove or disprove theories. Later, Galileo refers to those scientists who see that two and two equal four. Here Mrs Sarti is suggesting that Galileo is fanciful in his calculations. Galileo argues precisely the opposite when he puts his faith in reason supported by scientific experimentation and objectivity. Ludovico reiterates Mrs Sarti's suspicion when he says, 'You see, everything in the sciences goes against a fellow's good sound commonsense' (p.12).

The difference between what we see and what we think we see (and the connection to truth and reason) is a central idea of the play. It also helps us understand Brecht's desire to use the play as a teaching text: to help his audience critically view the world around it.

The commercial exchange of knowledge

This scene also demonstrates the commercial exchange of knowledge (how knowledge can be bought and sold). This is first highlighted when Galileo agrees to take on Ludovico Marsili, 'a rich young man' (p.11), as a pupil, even though Ludovico freely admits he is not much of a student. In contrast, Galileo jokes that the bright Andrea will have to drop out: 'You don't pay, see?' (p.12). The monetary value of new discoveries is further reinforced when Galileo welcomes the arrival of the university procurator, who explains that 'What is worth scudi is what brings scudi in' (p.15). As Galileo himself freely admits, this visitor 'matters' because an extra 500 scudi from the university will mean more time to spend on his research and less time having to 'bother' with pupils (p.13).

Freedom of thinking

Finally, the discussion between Galileo and the procurator reveals how important freedom of thinking is at this time when new ideas can be perceived as irreligious, even heretical, and therefore very dangerous.

Q How does this scene set up Galileo as an ambiguous character? Are audience members expected to sympathise with him? How ethical does he appear to be?

Q The university procurator suggests that some disciplines are more productive than others. What kinds of learning are valued in this text? Does this remain the same today? Might this have been different again when Brecht was writing his play? Why or why not?

Q What does the procurator mean when he says 'why investigate falling bodies, when it's the laws governing grovelling bodies that count' (p.16)?

Q How might the words 'GRACIA DEI' (for the grace of God) revealed through the telescope at the end of the scene be read as ironic?

Scene 2 (pp.19–22)

Summary: *Amidst much fanfare, Galileo presents 'his' invention of the telescope to the Venetian Republic. He passes off the design as his own even though he only learned of the invention through Ludovico's recent visit to Holland.*

Here the audience is positioned to question Galileo's code of ethics. The verse at the beginning of the scene draws attention to Galileo's taste for the good things in life and how this, in turn, affects his 'virtue' (p.19). While Galileo proudly claims the telescope as the result of seventeen years of research, he has merely re-created the Dutch invention (pp.20–1). The dramatic irony of Galileo's speech characterises him as the kind of man who will happily make compromises to achieve what he perceives to be the greater good or higher purpose. The Venetian Doge and the senators enjoy looking through their 'lucrative plaything' (p.20), which

Galileo views much more seriously as a means to proving Copernicus' theory.

Key point

Juxtaposition, in art or literature, is the useful technique of placing two different things side by side. The contrast can draw attention to an underlying or symbolic meaning. In this scene, the words and actions of the Venetian dignitaries are juxtaposed with the private conversation Galileo carries out with his friend Sagredo. As such, this reveals a great deal about the different characters' values, preoccupations and concerns.

Q What is the significance of the last line of the scene, Ludovico's reflection that 'it strikes me I'm starting to learn a thing or two about science' (p.22)?

Scene 3 (pp.22–34)

Summary: *Galileo, using the telescope, finds evidence to prove the Copernican system. Despite Sagredo's warnings about how this 'proof' might be perceived by powerful men in the Church, Galileo is adamant that reason will win out in the end.*

Again, the verse at the beginning of the scene points to the key idea here. In proving the Copernican system, as the last line reads, 'Galileo Galilei abolishes heaven' (p.22). In his study in Padua, Galileo shows Sagredo the proof that 'goes against 2000 years of astronomy' (p.23). Essentially, in disproving the Ptolemaic model of the cosmos, Galileo overturns the traditional religious conviction that God created earth as the centre of the universe.

However, Galileo shows himself to be somewhat naive, even pompously arrogant, when he so proudly pronounces, 'Today mankind can write in its diary: Got rid of heaven' (p.24). Further characterising himself as somewhat self-centred and indulgent, with a taste for the finer things in life, he says, 'Then I like buying books about other things besides physics, and I like a decent meal' (p.26).

Scene 4 (pp.34–43)

Summary: *Galileo has gone to the Court of Florence to show off his discoveries. The court scholars are dubious about these new ideas.*

This scene draws our attention to the different ways in which knowledge is constructed and valued. As Mrs Sarti cleans Galileo's study for visitors, she equates knowledge of the world with reading and 'sitting and poring over all that learning' (p.34). Mrs Sarti believes that the clergy can definitively pronounce Galileo's theories proven or otherwise because of the knowledge they have gained from books: 'If there was anything to all these discoveries the clergy would be the first to know' (p.34).

However, the later arrival of the university professors shows that those who can lay claim to knowledge and learning are not always best placed to judge 'truth'. These learned types do not wish to acknowledge evidence that is uncomfortable and difficult to negotiate. This is apparent when they refuse to see cases of plague in the city for what they are, instead attempting to reassure themselves that the illnesses are simply due to the common cold: 'Those cases in the old city: our faculty of medicine says there's no question of it being plague' (p.37).

Refusing to see

In his exchange with the nine-year-old Duke of Florence, Cosimo de Medici, Andrea highlights the same kind of problem. There is a disparity between what is 'known' (in the books of Aristotle) and what can be seen (via the telescope). Of the Ptolemaic system, Andrea says, 'That's how people think it is', but when he points to the Copernican system, he states: 'this is how it is really' (p.36). Symbolising the tussle for power between old and new ways of knowing and seeing, the model of the Ptolemaic system ends up broken after the boys' argument.

Significantly, reinforcing the idea of refusing to 'see', the philosopher and the mathematician refuse to look through the telescope. Rather than observing the stars Galileo has discovered around Jupiter, the philosopher wishes to first debate: 'Can such planets exist?' (p.38). This is a ludicrous suggestion that portrays the philosopher in a particularly unflattering light. The esoteric, unnecessary nature of the philosopher's proposed topics for debate stereotypically demeans the discipline of Philosophy. Nowhere is this more obvious than in the philosopher's questioning of whether such stars are necessary (p.39). When Galileo insists that the discussion continue in the vernacular rather than in Latin, the philosopher pompously (and foolishly) comments, 'The argument will be less brilliant, but it's your house' (p.39).

Galileo says to the Florentine scholars, 'go by the evidence of your eyes' (p.41) but they refer back to Aristotle and accepted ways of knowing or seeing things. As the mathematician says: 'My dear Galileo, I may strike you as very old-fashioned, but I'm in the habit of reading Aristotle now and again, and there, I can assure you, I trust the evidence of my eyes' (p.41). Dryly, Federzoni points out that Aristotle had no telescope (p.41). Here, then, we see how a lens-grinder can see what the clever scholar does not.

Key point

This makes Brecht's political point that ordinary people are more capable of seeing the truth of a situation than those who benefit from and are privileged by their authority and power. Further reinforcing the notion of the open-minded worker who judges according to observable phenomena, Galileo refers to draughtsmen, builders and instrument mechanics who 'don't read much, but rely on the evidence of their five senses, without all that much fear as to where such evidence is going to lead them ...' (p.43). Of course, the court intellectuals refuse such sensory evidence not because they are 'stupid' as Andrea suggests, but because they have a vested interest in the hierarchical structure of the universe due to the way this translates to an earthly context.

Q Why is it important that Galileo does not want to speak in Latin with the philosopher and the mathematician? What does this suggest about Galileo and his approach to sharing knowledge?

Q Consider the philosopher's argument about the danger of disrupting the harmony of the universe (p.39). What do you notice about the language he uses? How does it characterise the philosopher?

Scene 5 (pp.44–9)

Summary: *There is an outbreak of plague but Galileo ignores this to continue with his work. He sends Virginia and Andrea away but Andrea escapes from the carriage to return to Florence. Mrs Sarti refuses to leave Galileo and contracts the disease.*

The question of Galileo's motives arises out of his behaviour in this scene. When he is warned of an outbreak of plague in Florence, he refuses to leave with Virginia, Mrs Sarti and Andrea. He puts his research before the welfare of his daughter and those in his care (who are understandably upset that he is planning to stay behind). Even as Galileo rightly condemns the city officials for 'hush[ing] it all up till it was too late' (p.44) as alluded to in the previous scene, he does not act in the best interests of those for whom he is responsible. Illustrating precisely the opposite motivations, Mrs Sarti stays to look after Galileo. Furthermore, when Mrs Sarti realises she has contracted the disease she leaves Galileo's house to avoid spreading the infection and to ensure that his house will not be closed off; he can thus continue with his work.

There is further evidence in this scene of Galileo's obsession with his work. When Andrea returns to the city after a three-day walk, Galileo appears more focused on what he has proven (and on a chart he needs Andrea to fetch for him) than on Andrea's health or concern for his mother. In a rare moment of self-confession (at least up until this point in the play), Galileo interrupts his own theories about Venus to tell Andrea: 'I never asked for her to stay … But of course if I hadn't stayed myself it wouldn't have happened' (p.49).

Q Is Galileo working for the greater good when he continues his research or is he simply selfish? What evidence from the text can you cite to support your argument?

Scene 6 (pp.50–5)

Summary: *Galileo's research is validated by Christopher Clavius, the Church's greatest astronomer, at the Collegium Romanum (a Vatican research institute).*

In the hall of the Collegium Romanum, monks and scholars are having an hilarious time making fun of Galileo's ideas. This creates audience sympathy for Galileo who must patiently bear the insults directed at him and his theories.

Questions of faith

This conversation highlights why there is resistance to Galileo and a new model of the universe. For religious believers, questions about the solar system are equally questions about the Faith. The monk puts it this way: 'Which is better, I ask you: to have an eclipse of the moon happen three days later than the calendar says, or never to have eternal salvation at all?' (p.52).

Representing their faith in the literal truth of the Bible, the very thin monk and the very old cardinal are horrified by Galileo's claims that mankind and the earth are not at the centre of the universe. Amusingly, and none too subtly, the cardinal rants and rages about his significance at this centre before he collapses. This creates a moment of black comedy – the old cardinal's faith that he is made in God's own image contrasted with the evidence of his feebleness.

Towards the end of the scene Clavius utters only two words: 'He's right' (p.54). However, when the little monk suggests to Galileo that he has won, Galileo responds that 'reason has won' (p.54). Of course, winning or losing is never so simple, especially in a play such as this, and a significant exchange at the end of the scene reveals that the Cardinal Inquisitor (a cleric charged with investigating cases of heresy for the Church) is also investigating Galileo and his telescope.

Q What is the significance of Galileo's actions and words when he lets a stone drop to the floor?

Scene 7 (pp.55–63)

Summary: *Galileo attends a ball at Cardinal Bellarmin's house in Rome. Bellarmin tells Galileo that Copernicus' theories are heretical and warns him about keeping his research 'hypothetical'.*

Symbolically, Galileo questions the traditional and 'cramped' way in which the two secretaries are playing chess. He tells them that the chess pieces can now move more freely and adventurously, likening them to ocean explorers who no longer hug the coast. In this way, the Galileo of the play metaphorically points to the importance of unshackling the mind and allowing new ideas and possibilities free range.

With the arrival of Cardinals Bellarmin and Barberini, Galileo has further opportunity to reflect on moving beyond the previously accepted and safe confines of astronomical thinking. When Barberini quotes from the Scriptures in support of the sun's movement, Galileo responds by pointing out the difference between what is seen and what is perceived to be seen. Looking, seeing and understanding are not necessarily synonymous. In sharing his view that 'We must move with the times' (p.57), Bellarmin hypocritically suggests that while the Church accepts new knowledge helpful to commerce and trade, it will not welcome knowledge which undermines the Scriptures. To the same end, Barberini quotes scriptural passages. In a barely veiled reference to the Inquisition, Barberini cautions Galileo that he will be 'burned' if he ventures onto hot coals (where the coals represent dangerous knowledge).

Galileo shows in this scene that he is not adept in deception and political manoeuvring. In his blithe faith in 'reason' and the truth of his discoveries, he does not realise he has been deceived by the secretaries recording his conversations for the Inquisitor.

Key point

Demonstrating the corrupt and deceptive nature of officials in the institutional Church, the cardinals replace their masks after their frank conversation with Galileo. Barberini's advice, 'You too, my dear fellow, ought really to have come disguised as a good orthodox thinker' (p.61), implies that he disguises his own unorthodox thoughts behind an acceptable mask (indeed, earlier in the scene (p.58) he offered to point out ladies of 'international repute'). Although they carry masks of the lamb and the dove (representing innocence and peace), they are cunning and wily political manipulators. Most shockingly, Barberini says: 'Dressed like this I might be heard to murmur: If God didn't exist we should have to invent him' (p.61).

Q Why does this scene include the excerpt from the Lorenzo di Medici poem spoken in the background?

Q Why does Barberini relate the origins of Rome to Galileo? Is there a hidden message in the legend?

Scene 8 (pp.64–9)

Summary: *The little monk visits Galileo in Florence.*

Galileo reveals his increasing disillusionment with the Church and its decrees. When the little monk wishes to speak, Galileo cynically remarks that the monk's habit gives him the right to say what he pleases. In the same resigned, ironic way, Galileo informs the monk that his study of mathematics 'might come in handy if it led you to admit that two and two sometimes makes four' (p.64). Galileo is frustrated because his observations and Copernicus' model 'add up' and yet he is complicit in keeping this truth hidden. The audience can still appreciate something of the hero in Galileo as he contemplates being trapped in a dungeon if it will help him discover light. He is uncomfortable with keeping his discoveries under wraps: 'How long can I go on shouting it into the void, that's the question' (p.69).

The central theme of power is explored in this scene. For example, Brecht shows:

- The way in which the Church maintains its authority; the little monk refers to the Church's 'exceptional powers of enforcement' (p.64).
- The way the Church uses its power to wage wars in Germany and Spain (p.66).

- Galileo's response to Church power. The tone of his language here is more heated and militant, with a revolutionary flavour: 'Oh, to hell with it: I see your people's divine patience, but where is their divine anger?' (p.68).

Q The monk argues that the decree of the Holy Congregations reveals a 'noble motherly compassion' (p.66). How valid is this argument do you think?

Q Why does Cardinal Bellarmin's coachman bring Galileo gifts? How does this direct audience sympathy towards Galileo at this point in the play?

Q What is the origin of the phrase 'an apple from the tree of knowledge' and what is its significance in this scene?

Scene 9 (pp.69–81)

Summary: *Galileo has gained a reputation in the scientific world but for eight years has limited his research to 'floating bodies'. However, when he hears that Barberini, a mathematician, is likely to become pope, Galileo decides to once again study the heavens. In doing so, he alienates Ludovico who breaks off his engagement to Virginia.*

This scene opens and ends with Virginia. At the beginning she happily sews her trousseau with Mrs Sarti and talks about her forthcoming wedding to Ludovico. She is a picture of cheerful domesticity. However, at the end of the scene she faints in horror when she realises that her father has sent Ludovico away. Galileo's self-interested response, 'I've got to know', portrays him as a thoughtless and inadequate father as he goes on with his experiments (p.81).

Key point

An important moment in this scene occurs when Galileo condemns his former student Filippo Mucius because Mucius published work attacking Copernicus' theories. It's significant because Galileo is so quick to judge Mucius: 'someone who doesn't know the truth is just thick-headed. But someone who does know it and calls it a lie is a crook' (p.70). This is the judgement we must apply to Galileo when he later recants. As audience members then, we are positioned to see Galileo's actions as those of a 'crook'.

Galileo's weakness

When Ludovico reveals that Barberini is likely to become the next pope, Galileo immediately begins dreaming of taking up his forbidden research once again. Galileo's statement that 'Pleasure takes some achieving' (p.76) refers not just to the wine they have drunk, but also to the illicit pleasure of his intellectual pursuits: 'Knowledge will become a passion and research an ecstasy' (p.77). Losing all sense of caution and propriety, Galileo begins on his new sunspots project, work that Mrs Sarti pronounces 'devilish business' (p.77). Indeed, she likens Galileo's work to a dangerous addiction: 'two days of experiments and you're just as bad as before' (p.78).

This scene marks a turning point in the play. Firstly, the connection between the landowning families (the Italian aristocracy) and the Church authorities is made more explicit. The power and wealth of these ruling classes are interdependent and, as such, Ludovico explains that the next pope will 'have to take into account the devotion felt for him by the most respected families in the land' (p.78).

Q How does this scene illuminate class tensions and power relationships? How might this view of seventeenth-century society reflect Brecht's political views?

Scene 10 (pp.82–5)

Summary: *The carnival performance demonstrates how Galileo's doctrines have been taken up by the common people.*

The ballad singer sums up the significance of Galileo's ideas in terms of challenging accepted wisdom about the universe, and in turn, how this affects a religious world view and social structure. In claiming that the earth revolves around the sun, Galileo has turned the world upside down so that the greater now circles around that which is lesser (like a master around his servants).

Q The balladeer sings: 'People must keep their place, some down and some on top' (p.84). Investigate feudal society during the 1600s in Italy. How accurate is the singer's portrayal? What remnants (if any) of such a social structure are visible today?

Scene 11 (pp.86–90)

Summary: *Galileo refuses help from the cities of the north and faces the Holy Inquisition in Rome when the court of Florence announces it can no longer offer him its protection.*

Galileo's failing eyesight appears to be more than a physical ailment. It is also symbolic of his unwillingness to see the consequences of his controversial ideas. Tellingly, the previously sycophantic Gaffone (introduced in Scene 9) avoids Galileo at the beginning of this scene.

Vanni, an ironfounder from the north of Italy, tries to warn Galileo that he is being blamed for anti-biblical sentiment. In his arrogance, or wilful blindness, Galileo refuses to heed Vanni's warnings and does not accept his offer of help. Again, Galileo is a victim of his weakness of desiring a high standard of living (thus aligning himself with the aristocracy rather than the rising middle class) when he says, 'I like my comforts' (p.88). Galileo tells Vanni: 'I can distinguish power from impotence' (p.88), a statement that positions the audience to be critical of Galileo's choices in this scene.

Scene 12 (pp.90–4)

Summary: *The Pope and the Inquisitor discuss methods of dealing with Galileo's revolutionary doctrines.*

The Cardinal Inquisitor launches into a long and detailed diatribe against Galileo and his trust in reason. He argues that when humankind acts according to doubt rather than faith, God becomes unnecessary. Initially,

Pope Urban VIII (formerly Cardinal Barberini) responds to the Inquisitor's charges in a reasonable way: 'You can't condemn the doctrine and accept the charts' (p.93). However, as he dresses himself in the robes of his office, which denote his role as God's representative on earth, he becomes less of a scientist and more of an agent for the Church and its dogma. At the end of the scene, when the Pope is fully dressed and thus transformed (physically and metaphorically), he gives the Inquisitor permission to show Galileo 'the instruments' (p.94).

Q What is Galileo 'up to' and what is the Inquisitor suspicious of when Galileo 'writes his astronomical works not in Latin but in the idiom of fishwives and wool merchants' (p.92)?

Scene 13 (pp.94–9)

Summary: *Galileo recants.*

The actions of Galileo's friends and family illustrate the divide between a new age and the old. While Federzoni and the little monk play the modern style of chess Galileo advocated in Scene 7, his daughter Virginia kneels and prays. Importantly, Andrea is steadfast in his faith that Galileo will never recant. In a more pragmatic way, Federzoni is aware of what power can achieve and, possibly, of Galileo's weaknesses (p.95). Revealing the importance placed by Galileo's disciples on upholding 'truth', they are joyous when they believe he has not recanted: 'They embrace. They are ecstatically happy' (p.97).

For Andrea, Galileo's recantation is the ultimate betrayal. He clearly believes his hero has forsaken them all: 'Unhappy the land that has no heroes!' (p.98). It might be easier to align our sympathies with Andrea except that Galileo's entry is so full of pathos. He has been so affected by the trial that he is almost unrecognisable, and when his fellow scholars refuse to greet him he shuffles forward slowly because of his bad eyesight. Perhaps to counteract this moment of sympathy for Galileo, Andrea reminds us of Galileo's weaknesses – his desire for fine food, wine and knowledge: 'Wine-pump! Snail-eater! Did you save your precious skin?' (p.98).

Key point

Note the play of light and dark in this scene, where light represents an age of reason or 'enlightenment' and darkness superstition and falsehood. Federzoni comments that Galileo's recantation would have been 'Like nightfall in the morning' (p.97). Symbolically, as the crier calls out the recantation, Brecht directs that 'It grows dark' (p.98).

Q What does Galileo mean when he says, 'unhappy the land where heroes are needed' (p.98).

Q What is the purpose of the reading before the curtain at the end of this scene? Does Galileo's scientific prose counteract the sadness of the scene with its injection of rationality? Or is there a deeper meaning to this passage? Compare Galileo with the oak tree – could such a comparison reflect his own struggle maintaining the weight of greatness?

Scene 14 (pp.99–110)

Summary: *Galileo lives in the Florentine countryside, under house arrest.*

Despite attempts to portray Galileo as an anti-hero, moments of heroism shine through. At this point, Galileo is aware of his own wretchedness: 'I've been risking the last pathetic remnants of my own comfort by making a transcript' (p. 105). Immediately Andrea's faith in his hero is restored. He constructs an elaborate ethical argument to excuse Galileo's actions. Andrea refuses to see the truth of Galileo's recantation and Galileo, in the teacherly relationship he first demonstrated in Scene 1, tries to make Andrea understand that science has become the province of the wealthy and powerful.

Key point

This encounter between Galileo and Andrea echoes the first scene. However, in the first scene Galileo put off drinking his milk so that he could engage Andrea in passionate and joyous learning. In this scene, he lets Andrea go on his way so he can sit down to his food. Then it was morning and, symbolically, the dawn of a new age. Now it is the onset of night.

In this scene, at least momentarily, Galileo's revolutionary zeal is again evident:

> These selfish and domineering men, having greedily exploited the fruits of science, found that the cold eye of science had been turned on a primaeval but contrived poverty that could clearly be swept away if they were swept away themselves ... But can we deny ourselves to the crowd and still remain scientists? (p.108)

In denying himself to the crowd, Galileo no longer considers himself a scientist but, instead, one of the race of 'inventive dwarfs who can be hired for any purpose' (p.109). In another example of the ambiguity at the heart of his character, his speech about his betrayal of science's higher purpose is juxtaposed with his concern for earthly pleasures and weaknesses. As he finishes his speech of self-condemnation he says, 'Now I must eat' (p.109).

Q Galileo does not comment on the saying, 'When I am weak then I am strong' (p.101). Why not?

Scene 15 (pp.110–13)

Summary: *Andrea carries Galileo's manuscript, the Discorsi, out of Italy.*

The verse at the beginning of this last scene of the play speaks directly to the audience in a manner that seems appropriate to the purposes of Brecht's epic theatre. It entreats audience members to 'guard science's light' (p.110) and to use scientific knowledge and discovery for positive social purposes. The warning that the light could otherwise become 'a flame to fall / Downward to consume us all' (p.110) is a direct reference to the atomic bombs that engulfed Hiroshima and Nagasaki at the close of the Second World War. This knowledge of where modern science had ultimately led the world informed Brecht's revisions of the play.

In the conversation between Andrea, the frontier guard and the boys in the Italian border town, there is a significant play on the central theme of seeing, looking and (mis)understanding. The clerk and the guard do not see anything dangerous in the *Discorsi* that Andrea is reading. As the frontier guard notes, 'Nobody who wanted to hide something would put it under our noses like that' (p.111). Similarly, in response to their superstitious comments about witches and the devil, Andrea tells the boys, 'You should learn to use your eyes' (p.113). This piece of advice is for the audience as much as it is for the children.

CHARACTERS & RELATIONSHIPS

Galileo Galilei

Key quotes

'Today mankind can write in its diary: Got rid of heaven' (p.24).

'Thinking is one of the chief pleasures of the human race' (p.29).

'I believe in human reason' (p.29).

Galileo is a brilliant mathematician and scientist driven by his need to understand the laws of physics that govern the universe. He is so bent on his research that he fails to recognise its implications for the people around him, especially his daughter. Galileo is an ambiguous character. At the beginning of the play, the audience is positioned to see him as courageous as he takes on an authoritarian institution. Galileo at this point is a man of the people, seemingly dedicated to equality and intellectual exchange. He includes his lens-grinder in scientific discussions and he writes in the vernacular so that more people will have access to his ideas.

Yet, even in the first scene, Brecht wants to portray a complex character who is not simply 'good' or 'evil'. When Galileo jokes about tutoring students just for the money they will pay (rather than due to their intelligence or passion for the subject), he is depicted as a man more concerned with material comforts than with advancements and intellectual engagement in his field. His self-centredness is revealed when the boy Andrea must leave his coat with the lens-grinder as security. Not the slightest bit concerned, Galileo only asks, 'How will you manage without a coat this winter?' (p.18).

As the play continues, Galileo's actions begin to appear less heroic. Instead, he is presented as a flawed and self-indulgent man. He puts his passions before his daughter's happiness and he betrays the higher cause that he had previously so strongly advocated. His interests in science are presented as almost a vice, a dangerous addiction that does not allow Galileo to see beyond gaining people's acceptance of his opinions and beliefs. Ludovico puts this bluntly when he tells Galileo: 'You will always be the slave of your passions' (p.80). In some ways then, he epitomises the Brechtian 'anti-hero'. Ultimately, he sells out and compromises his principles because he is fearful of physical pain.

At the end of the play, however, it is difficult for the audience not to sympathise with Galileo. In stretching his poor eyesight to the limits to copy out his *Discorsi*, Galileo ensures that his knowledge can be shared. The audience is left with the question: Is this an act of an arrogant man keen to see his name live on forever, or is it an attempt to make up for his sins?

Q Is Galileo an easy character to read? What aspects of his characterisation do not 'add up'?

Andrea Sarti

Key quotes

'Unhappy the land that has no heroes!' (p.98)

'There are a lot of things we don't know yet ... We're really just at the beginning' (p.113).

Andrea is the son of Galileo's housekeeper and looks up to Galileo as a father figure and role model. In some ways, they are kindred spirits: impatient with those who refuse to attend to the evidence before them, and passionate about exploring and experimenting with new ideas. Andrea is quick to grasp the theories (and the evidence for these) as presented by Galileo, and he pursues studies of his own in the field of astronomy. Idealistic and naive, Andrea has Galileo on a pedestal and remains his loyal follower. He is confident of Galileo's commitment to truth, science and the pursuit of knowledge and therefore feels shocked and betrayed when Galileo recants before the Inquisition.

Significantly, Andrea is the vehicle through whom Galileo's work is disseminated when he carries the *Discorsi* across the border. At the end of the play we are presented with a more optimistic and buoyant Andrea, who once again has faith in the science he has come to love and defend. When one of the children at the frontier asks Andrea if people can fly through the air, he answers that, while it is not possible at present, a machine may be invented for such use in the future. His parting advice to the children, to use their eyes, echoes that which Galileo gave him at the beginning of his journey.

Mrs Sarti

Key quotes

'Let's hope your new time will allow us to pay the milkman, Mr Galilei' (p.10).

'I advised him to give the gentlemen a good supper ... before they inspect his tube' (pp.34–5).

'Do I serve your dinner or do you serve mine?' (p.30).

Galileo's housekeeper and Andrea's mother, Mrs Sarti is a down-to-earth foil for Galileo's intellectual pursuits. In terms of her class status, Mrs Sarti, as servant to Galileo, is largely inconsequential. However, she is wise in the ways of the world (perhaps more so than her employer) and sees clearly that people of lesser importance always circle those who are great. Despite her faith in astrology and her suspicion of Galileo's research, Mrs Sarti is unfailingly loyal to Galileo, ensuring that he is well looked after even at the expense of her own health; she demonstrates the selfless and sensible qualities he does not. Mrs Sarti speaks to Galileo candidly, perhaps signalling a more intimate relationship, when she says, 'you have no right to trample all over your daughter's happiness with your great feet' (p.78).

Ludovico Marsili

Key quotes

'I've not got the brains for science, Mr Galilei' (p.12).

'Nobody can drink a glass of wine without science these days, you know' (p.13).

'Marriages in families like ours are not based on purely sexual considerations' (p.77).

Ludovico is a wealthy young man who, at his mother's behest, seeks out Galileo's tutelage. Ludovico admits that he is not the brightest or most capable student but, because he can pay well, Galileo agrees to take him on as a pupil. Ludovico comes to represent the rich landowning class in sixteenth-century Italy. He is betrothed to Galileo's daughter Virginia but breaks this engagement, after eight years, when he discovers that Galileo is continuing to experiment in ways that undermine Church doctrine and beliefs. Appearances and reputation are important for Ludovico and his family, and the destabilising politics of Galileo and his work could tarnish the family name. Ludovico also makes clear the connection between the religious hierarchy and the support it receives from wealthy landowning families (p.78).

Mr Priuli

Key quotes

'If you want money you'll have to produce something else' (p.16).

'Once again a glorious page in the great book of the arts is inscribed in a Venetian hand' (p.20).

Mr Priuli is the procurator of Padua University, in charge of the university's finances. He suggests that Galileo needs to produce something practical from his research to justify an increase in wages. In this sense, Mr Priuli first introduces the idea that commerce and scientific research are interconnected. In his modes of speech and his interactions with Galileo, it is clear that Mr Priuli has a great sense of his own importance and this is reflected in his officious nature. He is proud of his city's progressive attitude towards new ideas; to a large extent, this viewpoint is bound up with the city's reliance on new industries and new money (where new inventions and ideas can make a considerable difference in terms of efficiency and income). Unlike the older, feudal model of society represented by Ludovico, Mr Priuli is a member of a new trade-based economy.

Sagredo

Key quotes

'It is a disastrous night when mankind sees the truth. And a delusive hour when it believes in human reason' (p.33).

'I am fond of science, my friend, but I am fonder of you' (p.33).

Sagredo is Galileo's friend and an enthusiastic supporter of his work. He admires Galileo's tenacity and intellect but can see what Galileo does not; he recognises the dangers of presenting research that disproves a universe based on a religious world view. Sagredo warns Galileo not to present his research findings in Florence because they will be poorly received. Sagredo appears only at the beginning of the play, in Scenes 2 and 3, with his appearance and his warnings to Galileo providing the audience with the background necessary to understand why Galileo's research might be so damaging to the Church. In spelling it out for Galileo, he also spells it out for us when he asks, 'where is God in your cosmography?' (p.28).

Virginia

Key quotes

'Virginia will soon have to have a dowry: she's not bright' (p.26).

'You are very kind, your Eminence. I really understand practically nothing about such things' (p.62).

Virginia, Galileo's daughter, is a pitiable figure. She is self-conscious, somewhat vacuous and eager to please. Her father seems to have little regard for her future. He regards her as lacking in intellect; he says she is 'not bright' and he refuses to allow her to look through his telescope because it is not a 'toy' (p.31). Highlighting the contrast between the ways in which he treats Andrea and Virginia, Galileo demands that Andrea be woken during the night so that he can look through the telescope (p.30). Virginia becomes a victim when Ludovico Marsili breaks off their engagement because of her father's ambition and arrogance (p.80).

Federzoni

Key quotes

'Mr Federzoni is a lens-grinder and a scholar' (p.39).

'How am I to doubt anything? How often do I have to tell you I can't read the books, they're in Latin' (p.72).

'This truly is the start of the age of knowledge. ... Imagine if he had recanted' (p.97).

Federzoni is a lens-grinder, Galileo's assistant and, in some ways, an agitator for change. When the Florentine philosopher tells Federzoni that any textbook will attest to the existence of the crystal spheres, Federzoni is pragmatic and even a little revolutionary in his response: 'Right, then let's have new textbooks' (p.41).

Federzoni's revolutionary zeal is again witnessed after Ludovico has departed in anger at the news that Galileo and his colleagues are 'starting up the earth-round-the-sun act again' (p.76). In a near-hysterical celebration of their research and its purpose, Galileo, Andrea and Federzoni farewell Ludovico. Importantly, Federzoni, in embellishing Andrea's goodbye, says the Marsilis 'command the earth to stand still so their castles shan't tumble down' (p.80). This remark reveals that some resistance to Galileo's theory is based on people's scepticism about a moving earth (wondering why we don't fall off the earth, as Andrea himself argues in Scene 1). More metaphorically, however, the castles can be read as signifying the power this kind of family wields. If science causes the workers to question the social order of things, families such as the Marsilis have a stake in ensuring that the earth stays still.

The little monk

Key quotes

'I couldn't see how to reconcile the decree I had read with the moons of Jupiter which I had observed' (p.64).

'God made the physical world, Ludovico; God made the human brain; God will permit physics' (p.78).

The little monk is caught between his passion for science and his love of God. He represents the central paradox of his age in terms of how he struggles to reconcile new scientific evidence and theories with his faith in the Bible and its literal translation. His conversation with Galileo in Scene 8 illustrates the relationship between the Ptolemaic system and the feudal hierarchy.

The little monk, like Galileo, cannot resist the lure of new knowledge. When Galileo shares his manuscripts, the monk must 'wolf it down' (p.68).

The Cardinal Inquisitor

Key quotes

'No mortal is so great that he cannot be contained in a prayer' (p.63).

'Practically speaking one wouldn't have to push it very far with him. He is a man of the flesh' (p.93).

The Cardinal Inquisitor is charged with investigating heresies against the Church. Naturally, then, he is interested in Galileo's research. When the Inquisitor meets Virginia he intimates that it is important to contain 'innovators' like Galileo: 'Yes, our innovators are living on a very grand scale' (p.63). As well as referring to the theories of people like Galileo, he refers to Galileo's fame and, therefore, to the spread of his ideas.

Many of the Cardinal Inquisitor's statements have double meanings, reflecting the duplicitous role he has in gathering information about people's heretical ideas and statements. For example, when he says, 'I am glad to know that you will remain close to your great father' (p.63) the Inquisitor is thinking of Virginia as an informant rather than simply as a loving daughter. Ultimately, it is the Cardinal Inquisitor who convinces the Pope to secure Galileo's recantation. The Inquisitor is concerned with maintaining the Pope's (and therefore the Church's) power base, which is reliant upon an existing view of the world – one with the earth and the Pope at its centre.

Cardinal Barberini (subsequently Pope Urban VIII)

Key quotes

'I suppose God hadn't got far enough in his studies before he wrote the bible; is that it?' (p.59)

Barberini is introduced in Scene 7 when he and Cardinal Bellarmin trade quotes from the Scriptures with Galileo at a ball at Bellarmin's house. Barberini reveals that he once studied astronomy and warns, 'It sticks to you like the itch' (p.57). He also shows that he is not above bribery: he makes a point of telling Galileo the legend of Rome so as to intimate how well looked after Galileo could be, before offering him 'ladies of international repute' (p.58). In this way, Barberini epitomises the rotten heart of the Church hidden beneath a mask of respectability and innocence (note the masks of the dove and the lamb). This helps to position the Church as a faceless and corruptible entity to be viewed negatively by the audience (in turn, evoking more sympathy for Galileo's fight against this authority).

In the ballroom scene, Cardinal Barberini is clearly sympathetic to Galileo's theories but he suggests that such sympathies are constrained by his religious dedication. Galileo does not understand this; he assumes that his scientific discoveries will be welcome when Barberini is appointed to the papacy. In an important scene, Scene 12, Barberini is robed. Just as Barberini is physically transformed by his robes, so too are his liberal attitudes toward Galileo's work. Although the Pope initially announces, 'Hands off him!' (p.93), his opinion changes when his robes transfigure him and he becomes an instrument of the Church's power.

Vanni (an ironfounder)

Key quotes

'... you're the man who's battling for freedom to teach what's new' (p.87).

'I sink or swim with people like you ...' (p.87).

Vanni is the voice of progress. He's significant even though he does not have a very big role in the play: he appears only in Scene 11. He is important because he offers a way out for Galileo, and hope for the future of science. Vanni recognises that Galileo is being blamed for anti-biblical sentiment in the wider community and understands that such a man will be considered dangerous by the Church authorities. With Vanni's cooperation (and the protection of other industrial interests), Galileo could continue his work at the boundaries of contemporary scientific endeavour.

Vanni's enlightened attitude is evident in his envious references to advances in other parts of Europe. His character helps to present Galileo as a potential hero for the ordinary people because Galileo fights a common enemy: the Church authorities. Vanni says, 'They're against ironfoundries because they imagine putting too many workers in one place leads to immorality. I sink or swim with people like you, Mr Galilei' (p.87). Unfortunately, Galileo is too proud and perhaps too elitist to align himself with what Vanni represents. He wrongly assumes that he is wanted only as a high-profile 'spokesman' (p.88). Distancing himself from the audience and making himself less heroic, Galileo dismisses Vanni's offer of support with a high-handed, 'I can distinguish power from impotence' (p.88). The audience therefore sees Galileo as informed by the same class system he claims to wish to change. At this point in the play, Galileo aligns himself with the ruling classes and we, as an audience, are therefore positioned to view him and his forthcoming actions rather more negatively.

THEMES, IDEAS & VALUES

Power

Key quotes

'... in chess too the rooks have begun sweeping far across the board' (p.8).

'... every ruler has his monks' (p.15).

'I was as strong as the authorities' (p.109).

'I handed my knowledge to those in power for them to use, fail to use, misuse – whatever best suited their objectives' (p.109).

The use and misuse of power is one of the central themes of *Life of Galileo*. The play explores this thematic concern through its focus on the struggle of an individual against an institution. Along the way, the audience sees how the Church maintains its authority via the connection between power and knowledge, and its ability to disseminate or suppress such knowledge.

Knowledge is power

Galileo, especially in earlier incarnations of the play, is portrayed as a figure of resistance who outsmarts an authoritarian regime. In seeking to share his knowledge of the universe, he is perceived as a threat to the institutionalised power structures in seventeenth-century Italy. Galileo is keen to witness a new age in which existing power relationships are turned upside down. The chessboard, and his interest in the ways in which the rooks can revolutionise the game, can be read as a metaphor for Galileo's intent to challenge the social order. Just as the chess player strategically uses rooks as part of a specific game plan, Galileo perceives that the ordinary people must lay siege to the higher social classes. To do this, Galileo attempts to share his knowledge publicly, producing work in the vernacular rather than in the more exclusive language of Latin.

Galileo envisions a world where access to knowledge is equitable, where 'Even the fishwives' sons will hasten off to school' (p.8). By the end of the play, the point is made even clearer. During Galileo's speech of self-condemnation in Scene 14, he bemoans his weakness: 'Had I stood firm the scientists could have developed something like the doctors' Hippocratic oath, a vow to use their knowledge exclusively for mankind's benefit' (p.109). Instead, of course, Galileo has spawned 'a race of inventive dwarfs', scientists who 'limit themselves to piling up knowledge for knowledge's sake' rather than using their knowledge to lighten the burden of human existence (p.108). If knowledge is power, the play argues, it should be shared among the many rather than limited to just a few.

The Church as the face of power

In the opening scene Galileo passionately explains to Andrea the model of a Copernican system of the universe, as well as excitedly pointing out the social ramifications of such an understanding of the world. Instead of the existing hierarchy, Galileo imagines a place in which the pope rolls cheerfully around the sun in much the same way as the fishwives, merchants, princes and cardinals. In other words, the Galileo of the play has a socialist vision for the future (clearly influenced by Brecht's own views and values).

In the first scene's triumphant and optimistic rendering of the future, Galileo predicts that the winds of change will reveal ordinary legs 'like our own' under the 'gold-embroidered skirts of the prelates and princes' (p.7). What he does not seem able to predict, however, is how zealously those in power will guard against ever allowing an ordinary person to catch a glimpse of the legs beneath those gold-embroidered skirts.

The way in which any authority wields and protects its power is therefore another thematic concern of the play. For Brecht, the Church represents just one face of authority and power in the world; the religious values of the institution are subsequently not as important as its ability to control and influence the society in which it exists. Galileo's interactions with the more powerful representatives of the Church (especially the Cardinal Inquisitor, Bellarmin and Barberini) reveal that it has the same interests as those of landowners like Ludovico. The drudgery of the peasantry against which Galileo rants in Scene 8 is just as crucial to the privileges and wealth of the Church as it is to the landowners. In this way the Church operates as a power structure: the ideological machine of the ruling class. It ensures that progress is stifled and that the people are kept docile and uninformed. The very old cardinal recognises in Galileo another member of the ruling class, hence his warning that sharing too much knowledge with underlings will have a detrimental effect on Galileo's own life of privilege and luxury. He angrily tells Galileo, 'you are fouling your own nest' (p.53). The Inquisitor also recognises in Galileo's work an inherent danger for the Church's authority and power. He sees 'the abolition of top and bottom' of society as the logical next step in a reordering of the universe (p.92).

As the play makes explicit, the Church, like most institutionalised power structures, has the means at its disposal to ensure that people do not speak out against an unfair lot in life. In this way, there are parallels with the secret police organisations and informer networks operating in authoritarian regimes such as Hitler's Germany. A number of characters warn Galileo about the ways in which the Church can protect its interests. In the first scene, the procurator reminds Galileo that Venice guarantees freedom of research whereas elsewhere 'any ignorant monk in the Inquisition could just put a ban on your thoughts' (p.15). In a more foreboding manner, Sagredo 'trembl[es] with fear' when he sees the truth of Galileo's evidence for a heliocentric universe (p.28). He reminds Galileo that Giordano Bruno had been burned at the stake for similarly heretical views. In the same vein, Mucius, Galileo's former student, defends his submission to the Church authorities with the line, 'there are worse things than the plague' (p.70). The little monk refers to 'certain exceptional powers of enforcement at the Church's disposal' before Galileo tells him to simply call them 'instruments of torture' (pp.64–5).

At the end of the play, in an statement which acknowledges that knowledge equals power, Galileo tells Andrea that he now realises he was as powerful as the Church. Unfortunately, he did not recognise this at the time (p.109).

Injustice

Key quotes

'Virtues are not an offshoot of poverty' (p.66).

'The poverty of the many is as old as the hills' (p.108).

'Yes, I might stir up his peasants to think new thoughts. And his servants and his stewards' (p.79).

Injustice, particularly in the forms of economic inequities and social divisions, is another important theme of *Life of Galileo*. Of course, the theme of injustice is also tied up with ideas about knowledge and education. Power and injustice are inextricably linked. Those who do not have any power are usually the same people weighed down by social injustice and inequality. Interestingly, although there are a number of references to the peasants at the bottom of the Renaissance food chain, *Life of Galileo* does not include any characters from the ranks of this lowly social class. This shows that, even in what might be termed a 'history play', the peasants are so inconsequential as to be referred to only in the third person. They have no voice in the text.

As a number of characters attest, the lives of peasants in seventeenth-century Italy are mainly marked by relentless toil and little reward. Ludovico refers to his peasants as 'beasts' and 'animals' (p.79). Indeed, like beasts of burden, he says they are kept 'busy in the fields' producing the rich cornfields wealthier men like Galileo observe from their coaches (p.79). When the little monk describes his parents, peasants in the Campagna, he paints a depressing picture of their bleak lives of poverty, disaster and hard work (p.65). Galileo promises a miracle for these peasants and for the working classes, those people who work with their hands in practical ways.

But, ultimately, Galileo does not deliver to these people (any more than do the Church leaders or rich landholders). Although he espouses efforts reflective of his high ideals, Galileo does not change things. At the end of the play, Federzoni has gone back to grinding lenses, the little monk has gone back to the Church and presumably the monk's parents continue to work in the fields in the Campagna in the same way as described in Scene 8. The inventions that might have made their lives easier – 'my new pumps will perform more miracles ... than all your ridiculous superhuman slaving' (p.67) – are sacrificed in Galileo's pursuit of a more intellectually 'pure', higher kind of knowledge. Paradoxically, it is Galileo's own class status as a rarefied intellectual (and therefore the way in which he is divorced from reality) that leads to his failure. Rather than providing life-furthering science for the people, Galileo delivers a death-dealing science for the ruling classes, a science in which a 'cry of triumph at some new achievement will be echoed by a universal cry of horror' (p.109).

Key point

Access to education and knowledge (or a lack thereof) serves to reinforce class divisions and injustice. In writing his own didactic plays for the masses, Brecht recognises this same link between redressing the social imbalance and sharing ideas and knowledge. Therefore, he has Galileo writing in the language of the everyday people rather than in Latin (which the lens-grinder Federzoni is at pains to tell us he can't read). The power of language to include or exclude, and to therefore reinforce the boundaries or layers of a hierarchical society, is a sub-theme of both power and injustice. As Galileo points out, 'The church's Latin ... protects its eternal verities from the curiosity of the innocent' (p.102).

Critical seeing versus mindless gawping

Key quotes

'Gawping isn't seeing' (p.9).

'... the man in the street concludes that a lot else might exist if only he opened his eyes!' (p.42)

'And no force will help them to make what has been seen unseen' (p.96).

The proper way of seeing and understanding is a central idea of the entire play, reflecting its thematic concerns with knowledge and power, and reinforcing values of truth and honesty. The play is dominated by astronomic observations and various references to the telescope, as well as comments on what the eye sees and what the brain perceives. Some characters see the truth but refuse to admit it (the Cardinal Inquisitor, for example, when he concedes Galileo's star charts are a necessary evil); some characters refuse to even look for the truth (the visiting scholars from the Florentine court who will not look into the telescope); while still others are frightened by the implications of what they see (Sagredo).

In some ways, the idea of seeing versus gawping (staring without thought or reflection) is a kind of motif: it is a repeated image and idea. We are first introduced to the idea when the play makes clear the opposition between right-seeing and wrong-seeing. When Andrea accepts surface impressions about the sun's daily movement: 'But I can see with my own eyes that the sun goes down in a different place from where it rises. So how can it stay still?' (p.9), Galileo is quick to condemn such thoughtless seeing: 'What can you see? Nothing at all ... Gawping isn't seeing' (p.9). Gawping, simply looking without a simultaneous commitment to critical viewing, is an abomination for Galileo. This reflects Brecht's own concerns with encouraging his audience to think about the themes and ideas in his plays rather than simply enjoying them as a pleasurable experience for the senses. Indeed, in a 1922 production of his play *Drums in the Night* banners strung in the theatre informed the audience not to 'gawp so romantically' (Rorrison 1986, p.xxxiv).

The play is concerned with making visible the invisible, whether this refers to the plight of the peasants, the machinations within power structures or the peaks and valleys on the moon. Importantly, there is more than a hint that right-seeing correlates with an alliance with the ordinary people. These people embrace new possibilities and new evidences. For example, when Ludovico dismissively refers to the way peasants hurry off to gossip when 'rumour says a pear has been seen on an apple tree' (p.79), he also reveals an openness to change that is not mirrored in the top levels of Church authority. Similarly, Galileo's work in the Venetian Arsenal (where ships are docked and loaded) shows him how draughtsmen, builders and instrument mechanics experiment with new approaches, relying 'on the evidence of their five senses' (p.43). Seeing properly, the opposite of gawping, combines theoretical knowledge with careful observation.

There are a number of other (interconnected) ways to consider the motif of seeing as a metaphor for 'true' understanding. The following bullet points will help you to further explore the idea of seeing and what it represents.

- Think about the significance of the telescope itself: all observation is 'mediated'; 'there is no self-evident, naked-eye truth any more' (Suvin 1990, p.189). How does this 'mediated' seeing connect to the idea of critical viewing? Whose lens(es) do you look through when you watch/read a text?
- Reflect on Galileo's blindness: how this develops from and emblematises his political blindness, and how this parallels the demise of his optimistic vision in Scene 1.
- Consider what we think we see versus what we are actually seeing: for example, Galileo's explanation of the ship and the shore (p.57)

and his demonstrations with the chair and Andrea in the first scene. Galileo encourages his pupils to think critically about evidence and preconceived and accepted ideas about the world. In the same way, Brecht encourages his 'pupils', his audience, to pay attention to what they see.

- Think about the significance of these contrasting structures: in the Ptolemaic system humans are seen by God whereas by using a telescope, humans can see the universe. How does this change the order of things in the world of the play?

Faith and doubt

Key quotes

'For where faith has been enthroned for a thousand years doubt now sits' (p.7).

'Our new art of doubting delighted the mass audience' (p.108).

Another important idea that appears throughout *Life of Galileo* is the central conflict between faith and doubt. Notice how in the first quotation above, faith is 'enthroned'; that is, it occupies a place of power and privilege. This idea connects to the theme of power as doubt can position the individual against the authority's accepted doctrines (heterodoxy versus orthodoxy). Clearly, during this play the audience is positioned to value the individual's right to freedom of inquiry, particularly given its implied parallels to a modern age.

The dramatised Galileo wants to spread scientific knowledge to the people; the historical Galileo was, in fact, a leader in publishing scientific work in the vernacular and he did respect the craftspeople of his age (Cohen 1970, p.87). However, critics have shown that Galileo was not quite so concerned with fishwives and Campagna peasants. As previously noted, Brecht's Galileo is heavily informed by a twentieth-century Marxist way of thinking. As Cohen puts it, Brecht's Galileo 'expresses more what science allegedly *ought to be* for the twentieth century than what it *was* for the seventeenth' (Cohen 1970, p.88). Therefore, Galileo's desire to bring science to the people is interlinked with a desire to spread doubt. This spirit of doubt, he believes, will result in the kind of revolution described in the opening scene.

Almost bookending the play, Galileo returns to the idea of doubt and scepticism during his self-critical outpouring to Andrea in Scene 14. Science, he says, demands courage because knowledge is 'procured through doubt' (p.107). According to Galileo, at the heart of this new science is scepticism of the old ways and superstitions, an attitude that might have freed the people. 'They tore the telescope out of our hands and trained it on their tormentors, the princes, landlords and priests' (p.108).

For Galileo, however, doubt has not entirely triumphed. Although pure knowledge has been gained and 'the battle for a measurable heaven has been won' (p.108), doubt has not been taken to its logical conclusion. Therefore, 'thanks to credulity', the ordinary people's lives go on much the same as before and 'the Rome housewife's battle for milk will be lost time and time again' (p.108). Here Galileo refers to the people's trust in the authority of the Church. Faith remains intact when the people should have learned to doubt the motives of the 'self-interested rulers' (p.108).

Key point

Historically, faith was increasingly challenged as people sought to understand the world through a rational, scientific lens. In Brecht's view, Galileo's discoveries about the universe marked a shift in thinking which radically altered society and which was a precursor to the enlightenment philosophy of the eighteenth century and, in turn, the Industrial Revolution of the nineteenth century.

Knowledge can be bought and sold

Key quotes

'Mathematics, so to speak, is an unproductive art' (p.14).

'When you're selling knowledge you can't ask more than the buyer is likely to make from it' (p.16).

'I sell out, you are a buyer' (p.107).

Life of Galileo explores the notion that everyone and everything has its price. Essentially, this means that knowledge (and the scientists as keepers of that knowledge) can be bought and sold just like any other commodity. This is a fairly depressing view of the world, particularly in terms of scientific ethics, but it does drive home the important message that there is a rather complicated relationship between new scientific developments and those who would use such developments to profitable ends. Such benefits or 'profits' can serve to strengthen an institution's power, not just its economic profits.

The links between scientific discovery and commerce are first signalled in Galileo's pleas for a wage increase during his conversation with the procurator of Padua University, in the first scene. When the procurator tries to explain that the people applauding Galileo's ideas don't pay the university what he costs it, he cynically responds, 'I see. Freedom of trade, freedom of research. Free trading in research, is that it?' (p.16). Although the procurator wisely advises Galileo that he should not underrate trade (p.17), this is precisely what Galileo does.

Indeed, in later refusing an offer of help from the ironfounder Vanni and his supporters in the north, the Galileo of the play seals science's fate. To some extent the play suggests that if Galileo had aligned himself with manufacturing interests (represented by the industrialist Vanni), he might have better evaded the clutches of the Inquisition and secured a better future for a science of the people. Vanni himself makes this connection: 'I think you'd be better off in Venice. Fewer clerics. You could take up the cudgels from there' (p.88). You may or may not agree with this line of argument, especially given a contemporary context. Do industrial and commercial interests use science any more responsibly than other authorities, such as governments?

Again, in Scene 3, in response to Sagredo's comment about the telescope's philosophical value, the procurator is quick to refocus the discussion on the commercial success of Galileo's water pump, irrigation system and weaving machine (p.25). Money-making science is the only kind in which the procurator is interested and when he leaves Galileo's study in anger, Galileo rightly points out that he is not so much upset about the honour (or otherwise) of Galileo's ruse with the telescope, but more because 'A world where one can't do business turns his stomach' (p.26).

At the conclusion of the play Galileo himself makes this link between commerce and science even more explicit when he welcomes Andrea, 'brother in science and cousin in betrayal', to 'the gutter' (p.107). Here Galileo uses the language of commerce: 'I sell out, you are a buyer. O irresistible glimpse of the book, the sacred commodity!' (p.107).

Truth and honesty

Key quotes

'If I were to agree to keep my mouth shut my motives would be thoroughly low ones: an easy life, freedom from persecution, and so on' (p.67).

'They're beheading the truth' (Andrea, p.97).

Life of Galileo makes its values clear by initially presenting Galileo positively, as a figure who bravely stands up for truth, honesty and integrity. As an illustration of how the association of values with particular characters enables Brecht to represent a contest of ideas, consider the fourth scene of the play, in which the Florentine scholars visit Galileo to investigate his telescope and the Medicean stars. The particularly unflattering characterisation of the Florentine philosopher (who is haughty, ego-driven and so narrow-minded as to appear stupid) ensures that we question his view of keeping the truth hidden lest it should lead somewhere unknown. In comparison to Galileo's calm, qualified statement that 'our duty as scientists is not to ask where truth is leading', the philosopher responds agitatedly (and therefore, almost pathetically), 'Mr Galilei, truth might lead us anywhere!' (p.42).

Significantly, the practical, loyal and honest lens-grinder Federzoni (also positively depicted in the play) reminds the scholars that as teachers they should be promoting questions rather than defending out-of-date knowledge and ideas (p.42). It is notable that the simple and honest Federzoni sees to the 'truth' or heart of the matter.

Later in the play, Galileo is portrayed in far more negative terms when he shows he does not have the courage to stand up for truth. In Scene 14, Galileo is scathing in his own self-condemnation. However, showing that, in the end, brute power cannot win out over truth, Galileo copies the *Discorsi* and Andrea carries this important scientific work across the Italian border.

DIFFERENT INTERPRETATIONS

Different interpretations arise from different responses to a text. Over time, a text will give rise to a wide range of responses from its readers, who may come from various social or cultural groups and live in very different places and historical periods. These responses can be published by critics and reviewers in newspapers, journals and books, both online and in print. They can also be expressed in discussions among readers in the media, classrooms, book groups and so on. A production of the play is also an interpretation of the text (the script).

While there is no single correct reading or interpretation of a text, it is important to understand that an interpretation is more than a personal opinion – it is the justification of a point of view on the text. To present an interpretation of a text based on your point of view you must use a logical argument and support it with relevant evidence from the text.

The many lives of Galileo

Given that there were three distinct versions of *Life of Galileo*, the play might be more appropriately called 'The many lives of Galileo'. This presents some interesting points for study. Rather than providing a single text that is produced and received in slightly different ways according to predominant social and cultural values, Brecht continually revised his play to better reflect what he saw as its main message or moral; it is 'the most heavily worked-over of all his plays' (Suvin 1990, p.188). Responses to this text have been somewhat contingent on which version is being viewed, read and discussed: it is therefore worthwhile to consider the play's inception and development in the hands of Brecht and his collaborators.

Brecht first wrote the play *The Earth Moves* in November 1938; he penned the play in just three weeks, but had been thinking about the character of Galileo and what he might represent for much longer. Later, with the assistance of Margarete Steffin, Brecht began to revise the play and in early 1939, the second version included a fourteenth scene and was given the new title, *Life of Galileo*.

In his original incarnation, Galileo is a positive 'anti-hero', one of a long line of this kind of hero in Brecht's plays. While Galileo recants, he is nevertheless a positive figure in his strategic, underground resistance to the Church authorities; he is presented more confidently as a man with a plan. In this original version, Galileo colludes with a stove-fitter to help him get the *Discorsi* out of Italy when Andrea serendipitously appears (Divay 2010). This change in plot and characterisation, though seemingly subtle, makes a considerable difference to how an audience might read or respond to the character of Galileo. In the original, Galileo shows considerable initiative and even a hint of bravery. This is a far more proactive Galileo than the character who simply copies his *Discorsi* at night but who seems to have no plan for its dissemination.

The original version of the play was performed for the first time in Zurich in 1943. Interestingly, even then the character of Galileo confused audiences (Rorrison 1986, p.xxii). Was his passive resistance a model for those intellectuals trapped within authoritarian societies, or was he simply a coward?

In the second, American version, Galileo's motives are made clearer and Brecht attempts a more pointed critique of his actions; it is no longer enough to passively resist and survive. Rather, Galileo is damned because he does not stand up and fight for the oppressed. The second version was written in the United States some six years after the original. Brecht, having witnessed many of the horrors of World War II by that time, collaborated with the actor Charles Laughton and made changes that more powerfully represented Galileo's betrayal of a higher principle. In Scene 9, the conversation between Ludovico and Galileo was developed to more obviously illustrate the hierarchical class structure in which Galileo had an opportunity to intervene. Similarly, Galileo's long speech about his own weaknesses appeared in Scene 14 to encourage the audience to view his character more critically.

The third and final version of *Life of Galileo* was a modified retranslation of the play on which Brecht and Laughton had collaborated a decade before. This play took the English version and translated it back into German. During rehearsals in 1956, the actor (Ernst Busch) who played the role of Galileo argued for a more sympathetic interpretation of his character. Indeed, a reviewer of the time said it was impossible to hate or condemn Busch's Galileo (Rorrison 1986, p.xxxi).

Key point

It is interesting to consider the original title of this play, *The Earth Moves*. How does it operate as a play on words? As well as referring to the scientific principle at stake for Galileo (a solar system in which the earth moves around the sun), could the title also refer to the ways in which old foundations of knowledge were shifting beneath people's feet? Could it be argued that the influences of so-called rational thought were once again destabilising the social order in the early twentieth century?

Interpreting Galileo

Given that the world around him was changing so rapidly as he revised and reworked the play, Brecht's vision for Galileo is never really resolved. Ultimately, Brecht does not seem to be entirely clear about who Galileo is and what he represents.

Apart from analysing the play's treatment of themes and ideas, there is another approach to considering differing interpretations of a text. This can be done by focusing on a particular character and how this character is 'read' and/or 'performed' over time. In this sense, Galileo's role is highly instructive as, in any performance of the play, it reveals the political stance a director takes when deciding whether to present Galileo more or less sympathetically to the audience.

Interpretation 1: Galileo is the hero of the play.

When Brecht originally wrote the play in 1938–9, he intended to present Galileo as the hero extolling rationalism and enlightenment. For Brecht, Galileo represented the much-maligned modern thinker striving for change against powerful forces of stasis and conservative thought. In the world of the play, Galileo triumphs because science will, in the end, serve the people. In this interpretation of the play, the Church functions as the authority against which Galileo's heroism can be played out; parallels can be drawn with the resistance to the rising oppression in Germany under Nazi rule at the time of writing.

In this light it is possible (though not necessarily easy) to excuse Galileo's recantation as a method of circumventing the Church authorities in a devious and clever way. (If he had simply sacrificed himself, the *Discorsi* would never have been completed.) This is the conclusion Andrea comes to when he says, 'If you had ended up at the stake in a halo of flames the other side would have won' (p.106).

Galileo's greatest crime, it would seem, is his decision to recant but it is possible to read his recantation more compassionately. Notably, in Scene 14, Galileo is transformed by his experience in prison. The stage directions read: '*Galileo has entered, so completely changed by his trial as to be almost unrecognisable*' (p.98). This invites audience sympathy and perhaps allows us to forgive him for betraying his ideals in the face of mental and physical distress.

Although Galileo is passionate about the good things in life (references to his taste in fine books, wine and food appear throughout the play), he is not so devoted to these things that he won't take risks. In the end, he does not act in the manner of a selfish, self-obsessed man seeking only his own pleasure. Although Brecht tries to portray Galileo's need to dwell on new ideas as an obsessive character flaw (a kind of addiction or vice), this does not quite add up. After all, Galileo copies the *Discorsi* at night, and given his failing eyesight and the hours at which he works, this is an intellectually and physically demanding commitment. It seems clear that he does this so that his work can be published for the benefit of all. Otherwise, why bother with the extra copy at night? According to this reading of the play, Galileo has outsmarted an oppressive regime and in the end, he does not place self-preservation before truth.

Interpretation 2: Galileo is the villain of the play.

In many ways, Brecht attempts to position the audience to see Galileo as the villain of the play – he constructs Galileo as a traitor and a liar. In the world of Brecht's play, Galileo cannot be redeemed because he promises his followers the conviction of his beliefs only to betray them. Due to his previously strident condemnation of others (such as his former student Mucius), his own about-face is made all the more terrible and horrifying for his followers and the audience. When Mucius arrives to speak with Galileo in Scene 9, Galileo says disgustedly: 'someone who doesn't know the truth is just thick-headed. But someone who does know it and calls it a lie is a crook' (p.70).

In this same conversation with Mucius, Galileo makes the point that concern for personal wellbeing should not impact on scientific work: 'I didn't let the plague stop me from recording my observations' (p.70). It is therefore more difficult to later excuse Galileo's recantation on the grounds that he was transformed by his trial. Galileo himself has already discredited such an argument.

As part of an audience we may feel moments of emotional sympathy with Galileo, but we can never completely forgive him. Brecht ensures this when he portrays Galileo's callous disregard for Virginia, despite her devotion and constancy. During his argument with Ludovico in Scene 9, Galileo offensively reduces his daughter to nothing more than her backside (p.77), and at the end of the scene when she faints, he does not move. Only 'Andrea and the little monk hurry to her side' (p.81).

Just as Andrea tries to excuse Galileo, the audience might also be tempted to explain his actions as a form of underground resistance. However, Galileo disabuses such a notion when he admits he was only concerned for his own survival. Brecht has Galileo confess his selfishness in his conversation with Andrea. Of course, Galileo is not just addressing Andrea when he says, 'I handed my knowledge to those in power for them to use, fail to use, misuse – whatever best suited their objectives' (p.109). He is also addressing us.

Finally, this penultimate scene reinforces the weaknesses in Galileo's character when he appears particularly concerned with food and eating. This can be read as a metaphor for his greedy self-interest; he gobbles down the goose liver that is brought to his room, more concerned with his stomach than science. Galileo's interest in the geese, particularly in who sent them, is significant at this point in the play. As bribes, gifts or, at the very least, signs of the good life of the upper classes, they symbolise the 'sell out' he has become (p.107).

QUESTIONS & ANSWERS

This section focuses on your own analytical writing on the text, and gives you strategies for producing high quality responses in your coursework and exam essays.

Essay writing – an overview

An essay on a literary work is a formal and serious piece of writing that presents your point of view on the text, usually in response to a given topic. Your 'point of view' in an essay is your interpretation of the meaning of the text's language, structure, characters, situations and events, supported by detailed analysis of textual evidence.

Analyse – don't summarise

In your essays it is important to avoid simply summarising what happens in a text:

- A **summary** is a description or paraphrase (retelling in different words) of the characters and events. For example: 'Macbeth has a horrifying vision of a dagger dripping with blood before he goes to murder King Duncan.'
- An **analysis** is an explanation of the real meaning or significance that lies 'beneath' the text's words (and images, for a film). For example: 'Macbeth's vision of a bloody dagger shows how deeply uneasy he is about the violent act he is contemplating – as well as his sense that supernatural forces are impelling him to act.'

A limited amount of summary is sometimes necessary to let your reader know which part of the text you wish to discuss. However, always keep this to a minimum and follow it immediately with your analysis of what this part of the text is really telling us.

Plan your essay

Carefully plan your essay so that you have a clear idea of what you are going to say. The plan ensures that your ideas flow logically, that your argument remains consistent and that you stay on the topic. An essay plan should be a list of **brief dot points** – no more than half a page.

- Include your central argument or main contention – a concise statement (usually in a single sentence) of your overall response to the topic. See 'Analysing a sample topic' for guidelines on how to formulate a main contention.
- Write three or four dot points for each paragraph indicating the main idea and evidence/examples from the text. Note that in your essay you will need to *expand* on these points and *analyse* the evidence.

Structure your essay

An essay is a complete, self-contained piece of writing. It has a clear beginning (the introduction), middle (several body paragraphs) and end (the last paragraph or conclusion). It must also have a central argument that runs throughout, linking each paragraph to form a coherent whole.

See examples of introductions and conclusions in the 'Analysing a sample topic' and 'Sample answer' sections.

The introduction establishes your overall response to the topic. It includes your main contention and outlines the main evidence you will refer to in the course of the essay. Write your introduction *after* you have done a plan and *before* you write the rest of the essay.

The body paragraphs argue your case – they present evidence from the text and explain how this evidence supports your argument.

Each body paragraph needs:

- **a strong topic sentence** (usually the first sentence) that states the main point being made in the paragraph
- **evidence** from the text, including some brief quotations
- **analysis** of the textual evidence explaining its significance and **explanation** of how it supports your argument

- **links back to the topic** in one or more statements, usually towards the end of the paragraph.

Connect the body paragraphs so that your discussion flows smoothly. Use some linking words and phrases like 'similarly' and 'on the other hand', though don't start every paragraph like this. Another strategy is to use a significant word from the last sentence of one paragraph in the first sentence of the next.

Use key terms from the topic – or synonyms for them – throughout, so the relevance of your discussion to the topic is always clear.

The conclusion ties everything together and finishes the essay. It includes strong statements that emphasise your central argument and provide a clear response to the topic.

Avoid simply restating the points made earlier in the essay – this will end on a very flat note and imply that you have run out of ideas and vocabulary. The conclusion is meant to be a logical extension of what you have written, not just a repetition or summary. Writing an effective conclusion can be a challenge. Try using these tips:

- Start by linking back to the final sentence of the second-last paragraph – this helps your writing to 'flow', rather than just leaping back to your main contention straight away.
- Use synonyms and expressions with equivalent or similar meanings to vary your vocabulary. This allows you to reinforce your line of argument without being repetitive.
- When planning your essay, think of one or two broad statements or observations about the text's wider meaning. These should be related to the topic and your overall argument. Keep them for the conclusion, since they will give you something 'new' to say but still follow logically from your discussion. The introduction will be focused on the topic, but the conclusion can present a wider view of the text.

Essay topics

1. 'Andrea's final caution to "learn to open your eyes" isn't just directed at the children at the border, but also at the audience members.' Discuss.
2. '*Life of Galileo* shows that ideological struggles are at the root of all conflict.' Discuss.
3. How does Brecht use symbols, setting and characterisation to portray the theme of injustice in his play *Life of Galileo*?
4. "How can there be people so perverse as to pin their faith to these slaves of the multiplication table?" Why is it so difficult for the very old cardinal to accept the ideas presented by Galileo?
5. '*Life of Galileo* presents a meditation on power in its exploration of authority versus the individual.' Discuss.
6. Galileo evolves from a brilliant all-seeing scientist to a nearly blind outcast. What does this mean for the brave new world he exultantly proclaims at the beginning of the play?
7. '*Life of Galileo* shows that having courage in the face of persecution is a universal human challenge.' How does it do this?
8. 'The social responsibility of the scientist is the moral of the play.' Do you agree?
9. '*Life of Galileo* is a timely parable for any age.' Discuss.
10. How do Galileo's domestic relationships with Andrea, Virginia and Mrs Sarti reveal the complexities of his character?

Vocabulary for writing on *Life of Galileo*

Epic theatre: incorporates the use of techniques such as summary projections, few props, visible stage machinery and 'cool' or estranged acting. It invites the spectator to use reason to reflect upon the performance (rather than to simply be carried away by the emotion of it).

Inquisition: established in Rome in 1542, this tribunal, composed of six cardinals, had the task of combating and suppressing heresy.
Parable: a story that illustrates a lesson.
Naturalism: originally a theatrical movement in the late nineteenth to early twentieth centuries, with quite specific guidelines (covering content as well as style). Naturalism has come to be used as a general term to describe a realistic style of writing/performance. In his work, Brecht challenged the conventions of naturalism in the theatre.

Analysing a sample topic

'*Life of Galileo* shows that ideological struggles are at the root of all conflict.' Discuss.
This is a deceptively simple essay topic. Sometimes these are the kinds of topics we are tempted to address because they seem so straightforward. Beware of making such an assumption. This topic requires a detailed knowledge of the play and its themes, as well as the sophisticated ability to write a succinct, purposeful essay in response.

Firstly, consider the key terms and phrases: 'ideological struggles', 'at the root of' and 'conflict'. It is important to 'unpack' the meanings of these words because this will clarify how you will frame and respond to them in your essay.

To what kinds of ideological struggles does the statement refer? To answer this question, you need to make sure you understand the meaning of ideology and how this relates to the play. If ideology can be taken to mean the ideas and manner of thinking characteristic of an individual or group, how does Galileo's way of thinking contrast with that of the Church? Importantly, because the Church is an institution, which characters will you choose to analyse in your essay to best represent the institution's ideas?

Similarly, conflict can mean many things. Does the topic refer to conflict between individuals or between different beliefs and value systems? Could it be an inner conflict (the conflict within an individual)?

Finally, consider that the topic includes a figure of speech – the phrase 'at the root of'. When we say that something is 'at the root of' a problem we mean that it is the origin or the underlying cause of the problem. So an issue to address here is the significance of the term 'root' (its association with something deeply buried, intractable and inflexible, and therefore, the often negative connotations it carries).

It is useful to paraphrase the topic and in doing so, to consider the subtleties of how the meaning of the statement changes in the process. This helps to frame a contention in the next step of the planning process. For example, consider the variations here: 'differences in ideology are the source of all conflict'; 'ideological struggles are the main cause of any conflict'; 'ideological struggles always result in conflict'. There are a number of possibilities. In paraphrasing the statement, note that you can qualify the *amount* of conflict caused by differences in ideology. Do ideological struggles lead to *all* conflict in the play? Or only *some* of the conflict? Or, indeed, are they the *most important* source of conflict?

After paraphrasing the topic consider whether you wish to argue for or against the statement. It is possible to sit on the fence and hover somewhere in between, but this is much harder to manage successfully. Often, disagreeing with a topic can be most interesting, but it may require more sophisticated skills in textual analysis and the ability to structure your argument particularly effectively. If you disagree, you might argue that while ideological struggles do cause a great deal of conflict in the play, other factors (such as fear and betrayal) are also causes of conflict.

In the outline below, the response agrees with the essay topic. The main contention of the essay is stated in the final sentence of the introduction.

Sample introduction

> *Life of Galileo* illustrates a great struggle between an individual and authority. The fundamental cause of the conflict is the difference in ideologies represented by the character of Galileo

and the dogma of the Catholic Church. Certainly, both parties involved in the central conflict have radically different ways of thinking about the world. Galileo has a scientific, rational approach to viewing the world, but for the Church, represented in key characters including the very thin monk, the very old cardinal and the Cardinal Inquisitor, such a way of thinking leads to blasphemy and heresy. There is no place for doubt in their world view. While the struggles between these different ideologies are not the only source of conflict in the play, the battle of ideas between Galileo and the Church is at its heart.

Body paragraph 1

- Focus on the character of Galileo first. What are his ideas about the world and how do these ideas conflict with the Church's view? (Look to Scene 1 for the earliest examples of Galileo's ideas and ways of thinking. What examples are there that these ideas will challenge the Church and its ideas about truth?)
- Even Mrs Sarti points out that Galileo's ideas are problematic (in that they are corrupting her son and she is having to explain Andrea's controversial ideas to the priests): 'You surely can't tell him such stories? Making him trot it all out at school so the priests come and see me because he keeps coming out with blasphemies' (p.10).
- In Scenes 2 and 3, Sagredo also spells out for the audience the reasons Galileo's ideas might be disagreeable to the Church.

Body paragraph 2

- Who are some of the characters in the play who represent the Church and its ideologies? Focus on these characters next.
- Scene 6 provides a wealth of characters and quotations that demonstrate why Galileo's scientific rationalism is so fundamentally opposed to their beliefs.

- The very thin monk and the very old cardinal are interesting characters on which to focus because they take the Scriptures quite literally (as this is the basis of their faith). For example, the monk rather anxiously argues: 'How can the sun stand still if it never moves at all as suggested by this heretic? Are the Scriptures lying?' (p.52).
- Significantly, the old cardinal highlights how ideologies are socially constructed. He shows how we 'learn' to think about the world around us: 'Mankind is the crown of creation, as every child knows' (p.53).

Body paragraph 3

- Having considered both sides of the ideological struggle through some key characters and the ideas and ways of thinking they represent, move the focus to the conflict between them. The carnival scene might be useful here as a way of exploring how the conflict is perceived in the world of the play.
- Then analyse the most dramatic moment of conflict between the two opposing world views. This is probably the scene in which the Cardinal Inquisitor persuades the Pope to silence Galileo through the sight of the torture instruments.
- The scene shows that the conflict between these opposing sets of ideas is deeply serious. It is no mere 'struggle' for hearts and minds, but a matter of life and death.

Sample conclusion

> The play illustrates how radically different ideological positions are at the root of conflict. The clash in ideologies is signalled at the outset of the play when Galileo naively puts his trust in reason. Throughout the play, the central conflict between the authority of the Church and Galileo's advocacy of his scientific discoveries is returned to repeatedly. Ultimately, the inquisition forces Galileo to recant and he publicly denies his ideas in

a terrible betrayal of his own values and belief systems. Here the conflict becomes one of life and death; it also becomes an internal conflict as Galileo struggles to accept the implications of what he has done. Underlying these conflicts is the clash of ideologies, the mutually incompatible world views of inflexible faith and scientific reason.

SAMPLE ANSWER

In *Life of Galileo* the central character evolves from an all-seeing brilliant scientist to a nearly blind outcast. What does this mean for the brave new world he exultantly proclaims at the beginning of the play?

Galileo's personal journey in the play *Life of Galileo* parallels the demise of the new world he so proudly proclaims at its outset. At the beginning of the play, Galileo, a brilliant scientist with a gift for 'seeing' the truth of things, is delighted to discover evidence to support the Copernican model of the universe. He sees this new understanding of the world as heralding a new social order based on equality and reason. However, as time passes and as Galileo encounters increasingly powerful resistance to his ideas, both his eyesight and his dreams begin to diminish and fade. Although Galileo declares the advent of a new world when he first looks through his telescope, by the end of the play he realises that the betrayal of his own ideals has consigned such a vision to history.

The play begins by focusing on what Galileo can see compared with what others cannot see. His ability to 'see' is meant in both literal and metaphorical senses. Through the use of empirical scientific methods and via the telescope, Galileo obtains the evidence necessary to support his theories. In a figurative way too, Galileo can see the truth of things; he is an enlightened, rational man. This is important because it establishes a clear connection between Galileo's scientific discoveries and his revolutionary ideas for society. It also establishes the motif of seeing as a metaphor for proper understanding. Galileo illustrates this for ten-year-old Andrea in the first scene: 'Everyone says: right, that's what it says in the books, but let's have a look for ourselves'. Indeed, when Mrs Sarti questions what they are up to, Galileo replies that he is 'teaching him to see'.

The world that Galileo teaches Andrea to see is vastly different from the one they inhabit. It is a world in which astronomy is discussed in the marketplaces and where men of a hundred wish to hear of the latest discoveries. Most dramatically, in this triumphant new world, the old order of things no longer exists. Breaking out of the 'crystal sphere' and its hierarchical order is an exciting prospect for Galileo. This new time will be 'a pleasure to live in'. Yet even in the first scene Galileo has some appreciation of how dangerous it may be to see the world in the way he does. He warns Andrea not to talk to other people about their ideas because the 'big shots won't allow it'.

When the 'big shots', the Church authorities, act decisively to counter Galileo's revolutionary ideas it is because they cannot allow his vision to survive. By this time, Galileo's eyesight is already beginning to fail. Things have been stagnant for too long (after he agreed not to pursue his research of the Copernican system) and he is losing sight of the brave new world he promised. When the Inquisitor and the Pope agree that Galileo must recant, it is significant that they both understand that just a glimpse of the torture instruments will expedite this end. After what he sees before him decides his betrayal, Galileo's journey towards blindness quickens. His descent into physical darkness begins at the moment he betrays the truth he had first seen through the telescope. As this darkness begins to descend on his eyes, it also closes in on the bright new world he had foreseen.

At the end of the play, the optimistic scientist has been reduced to a shadow of his former self, an almost blind man living in isolation at the edge of society. On his journey to this point he has also lost sight of his vision for a fairer society. Although he had first proclaimed a new age in which science would relieve the people of the burdens of their daily lives, science has not delivered. Instead, Galileo has become the father of a 'race of inventive dwarfs who can be hired for any purpose'. In this way, science has become another servant of the ruling classes and the people are denied the new world of equality and reason he had envisioned at the play's beginning.

REFERENCES & READING

Text

Brecht, Bertolt 1986, *Life of Galileo*, trans. John Willett, Methuen Student Editions, London.

Rorrison, Hugh 1986, 'Commentary', in Bertolt Brecht, *Life of Galileo*, Methuen Student Editions, London.

Books

Bentley, Eric 1965, *Parables for the Theatre*, Penguin Books, Middlesex.

Stanton, S. & Banham B. 1996, *The Cambridge Guide to Theatre*, Cambridge University Press, Cambridge.

Journal articles

Cohen, M. A. 1970, 'History and Moral in Brecht's *Life of Galileo*', *Contemporary Literature*, Vol. 11(1), pp.80–97.

Suvin, D. 1990, 'Brecht's Parable of Heavenly Food: *Life of Galileo*', *The Brecht Yearbook*, Vol. 15, pp.188–205.

Websites

Divay, Gaby 2010, 'Brecht's *Life of Galileo*: socio-political considerations', e-Edition, accessed 26 November 2012, http://home.cc.umanitoba.ca/~divay/ps/brechtGalileo84.html

'Inquisition' in *The Catholic Encyclopedia*, http://www.newadvent.org/cathen/08026a.htm

Johnston, Brian 2013, *Courses in Drama*, http://www.coursesindrama.com/ (a useful site with a section on modern drama and Brecht's *Life of Galileo*)

The Galileo Project, http://galileo.rice.edu/galileo.html (a hypertext resource on the life and work of Galileo Galilei)